ULTIMATE FOC
MASTERING CC

UNLOCK THE SUPERPOWER OF THE ULTRA SUCCESSFUL [IN 3 PHASES]

CHANDLER KITCHING

© Copyright 2020 - Chandler Kitching - All rights reserved.

The contents of this book may not be reproduced, duplicated or transmitted without direct written permission from the author.

Under no circumstances will any legal responsibility or blame be held against the publisher for any reparation, damages, or monetary loss due to the information herein, either directly or indirectly.

Legal Notice:

This book is copyright protected. This is only for personal use. You cannot amend, distribute, sell, use, quote or paraphrase any part or the content within this book without the consent of the author.

Disclaimer Notice:

Please note the information contained within this document is for educational and entertainment purposes only. Every attempt has been made to provide accurate, up to date and reliable complete information. No warranties of any kind are expressed or implied. Readers acknowledge that the author is not engaging in the rendering of legal, financial, medical or professional advice. The content of this book has been derived from various sources. Please consult a licensed professional before attempting any techniques outlined in this book.

By reading this document, the reader agrees that under no circumstances is the author responsible for any losses, direct or indirect, which are incurred as a result of the use of information contained within this document, including, but not limited to, — errors, omissions, or inaccuracies.

Dedicated to my beloved mother & father

Contents

My Ultimate Focus Tool Kit   6

Introduction   9

Phase 1: Master Your Brain, Body, and Environment

1. Programming Your New Mind of Focus   17
2. Habits - Automating Your Life for Success   33
3. Distractions – The Silent Killer of Dreams   49
4. Optimize Your Workspace for Peak Performance   61
5. Prime Your Biology for Focus   75

Phase 2: Focusing Deep - Starting Your Day of Ultimate Focus

6. How to Plan Your Perfect Routine for Ultimate Focus   91
7. Distraction is Not Evil   101
8. The Deep State – The Mystical State of Achievement   107
9. Mental Energy Management – The Art of Simplicity   115
10. Embrace Discomfort – The Way of the Warrior   129

Phase 3: Hacking & Advanced Focus Training Secrets You Need to Know

11. Mind Hacking – Decoding Dopamine   143
12. Brain Training Exercises to Build Monk-like Focus   153

Afterword   165

My Other Books You'll Love   169

References   170

MY ULTIMATE FOCUS TOOL KIT

(NEVER WASTE ANOTHER DAY WITHOUT THIS..)

As a way of saying thanks for reading my journey to concentration mastery, I would like to offer you my complete ultimate focus checklist for free.

My checklist includes:

1. 11 elegant tools to unlock your personal master focus plan.

2. My personal external brain arsenal for maximum efficiency.

3. My favorite subliminal & isochronic tone sources
for deep concentration.

This is the list I wish I had at the beginning of my journey to true attention.

To receive your ultimate focus tool kit, visit my web page or scan the QR code with your phone:

https://chandlerkitching.activehosted.com/f/1

INTRODUCTION

We live in a world of exponential transformation in a gushing stream of novel information. Concentration in a reality of excess stimuli is becoming the long-lost art of the pre-internet era. Our ancestors were hard-wired for distraction. It kept them alive in an age of predators. In the age of information, distraction has become the predator hunting all knowledge workers. It is our choice whether we utilize the tools at our disposal for focus or distraction. Most society is acquiring a Ph.D. in the dojo of distraction. We become exceptional every time we resist plunging into the urge of a notification. By reading this book, you have made the best decision for your life and career. To acquire your next level of success you require the ultimate focus tool kit.

This book is divided into three phases and twelve practical steps, which will help you regain control of your brain, environment and self-satisfaction. Most of society's issues are caused by the inability to prioritize what is essential. To achieve this goal, this book will cover every mental hack necessary to cultivate a life of sacred singularity and focused fulfillment. Phase one contains the most manageable first steps to take control of your brain, habits, environment, and biology. The next is phase two, which elaborates on how to begin your day of ultimate focus, plan your routine, manage your day, enter the deep state, and manage mental energy while increasing your energy threshold. The last phase will uncover the art of mind hacking, along with advanced focus exercises that will cut your journey to concentration in half.

All these techniques are deeply tested methods based on the experience of my colleagues and myself. I struggled with staying focused and was told by medical professionals that my brain was biologically deficient. Throughout grade school, I needed to work more hours than my classmates to get the same test scores. They diagnosed me with attention deficit disorder. I was told that I couldn't focus, and my brain had a deficiency according to medical professionals. They put me on
prescription drugs just to be "normal" like my classmates. I was rapidly losing weight from the medication, so my psychiatrist prescribed me milkshakes to gain back the weight. I know this sounds strange, but he did. Even as a kid, I knew that something was not right with the recommendations of my authorities. I stopped taking the stimulant prescription and began taking an SNRI for focus. It worked well, or at least I thought it did. Over those six years of taking it during high school and college, I forgot what my life felt like before the medication. If I ran out, I had thoughts of feeling hopeless in life, which is a classic symptom of SNRI withdrawal. I hated feeling out of control. They
tied me to this drug, and without it, I had no focus and felt sad for no apparent reason. Many individuals get significant benefits from attention medication however I felt out of control. I wanted to fix the root of my attention deficit. I slowly weaned myself off of the drug, which was incredibly difficult. I relapsed a few times because I couldn't bear the feeling of my brain feeling broken, especially at my various jobs. To overcome my feelings of deep dissatisfaction, I had to pursue mastering my concentration.

How this book will help you:

You will have the tools to master previously strenuous tasks swiftly by transforming the neural structure of your brain through the techniques I will share with you in this book. You will learn how to harness neuroplasticity to focus longer and deeper every day. We no longer have to struggle with mediocrity, missed deadlines, angry bosses or frustrated spouses. You will have the tools to blast off in your career and rediscover lost free time by gaining control of your focus. We will ditch the victim mentality, indoctrinated to us through our environment to build a deeply satisfying, joyful life for ourselves and families. Through this book, you will spend more time with your friends, family, passion projects and hobbies. If you have children, you will be present for all the milestones of their lives. You can finally fall in love with your life and experience every second to the max. Your life will become deeper when you simplify down to what truly matters.

This book will teach you how to control your distractions and utilize your work breaks; work deeply and rest deeply. By the time you reach the end of this book, you will have many tricks up your sleeve for achieving the lifestyle of your ultimate reality.

I started going to a doctor of psychology who gave me a user manual for my unfocused brain. The key lesson that she taught me was that to master my career and life, I have to master my brain. This sparked my lifework and journey of discovering the ultimate focus system. For the last 13 years, I have been perfecting my craft. I have made researching, experimenting and interviewing focused professionals as my life's work. I now have no problems with deeply focusing for 12 hours or more at a time. I can pursue my research, study, work my dream career, exercise, and have plenty of time left over for being with my family. I want to share my results with the world. I want you to be the master of your brain and captain of your life destiny.

With this 3-phase training system, I know that you will be fully prepared to cultivate your life of focus, unlocking your full potential and dream career.

There is a grave opportunity cost of not regaining control of our focus. We will fall behind in life and never have the satisfaction of a productive yet thrilling recreational life. I can vouch for this because I have been there in the past. My relationships inevitably suffered from working long hours without managing my time. Whenever I think about what happiness means to me, I remember the importance of being able to live every moment to the fullest. I want to be there to raise my kids and give them the best memories of spending time with their Dad. When my son is playing a baseball game, I want him to look into the crowd and see me there ready to support him no matter what my career throws at me.

When we are deeply focused, we show our employers we are of such significant value they can't afford to lose us. If you're an entrepreneur, your customers will value your service or product more which can lead to a cascading avalanche of success. I want your work to make a difference in your company. I want you to get compensated for your deep focus exponentially. I want you to let go of feeling drained to the point of having nothing left to give your loved ones after work.

You can find deep meaning from your work and life again. Achieving your dream life does not have to feel like Chinese water torture. Through this book, you can cultivate a zen warrior mindset that can conquer any hurdle.

My three-phase system has proven to increase focus, cognition, and learning. At the end of every chapter, you will find a list of actionable steps you can follow for exact applicable instructions on implementation. This book is low on theory and high on real-life practicality. You will find information backed by case studies and stories of high achievers from every walk of life. I have also included the most modern, innovative techniques of attaining focus, making this book one of the most comprehensive guides for mastering concentration with the highest quality tools.

Observe and execute every method in this book with an open mind. Try each of them to determine what works for you. Your ability to master all these techniques is equal to the effort you put into them. Your mind is a powerhouse of change. At the end of your journey, the power that your mind wields will surprise you.

PHASE 1: MASTER YOUR BRAIN, BODY, AND ENVIRONMENT

1

PROGRAMMING YOUR NEW MIND OF FOCUS

"The mind is everything. What we think we become."

SIDDHARTHA GAUTAMA BUDDHA

Trees are replaced with towering buildings and outdoor games with smart-phones. Technology is reshaping the world around us at an accelerated rate higher than any other time in history. That is why we must curate our daily information intake intentionally to program our daily thoughts and beliefs. This, forms how our brain is physically structured.

Habits are actions that we develop to automate our brain to consume less energy. These actions are repeated, to create a neural pathway. As each thought is repeated it becomes a habit and is ingrained in our psyche. Cultivating high quality habits and watching the information we feed our minds enables our brain to be any way we desire.

Understanding Neuroplasticity: The Key to Empowerment

Neuroplasticity is the brain's ability to form new neural pathways and synaptic connections from thoughts, actions or beliefs. This means that your brain can grow and learn new skills just by changing how you react to your environment. On the flip side if our inner and outer environment is not carefully selected then our brain can deteriorate, create synaptic connections for distraction and even lower our IQ. The power of action is increased by how many times it is repeated in a day and compounds over a lifetime. Eventually, repetition of any thought, action or belief leads to its perceived permanence as an involuntary automatic response of your brain. As more time passes repeating a certain thought or action, the more energy it will take to be conscious of it and eventually change. Therefore, you are literally transformed into your thoughts and actions which create the life of your wildest dreams or an eternal struggle.

Through the course of your lifetime, neuroplasticity will constantly shape you. Your brain is an organized web of interconnections. Some parts become stronger or weaker over time, based on whether they are being activated frequently. The younger you are, the easier it is for your brain to change because the synaptic connections are not as deeply ingrained. Neuroplasticity is traditionally thought to have been contingent on your age. However, more and more research suggests that with the proper care we can utilize neuroplasticity at any age. For instance, older individuals have been thought to find it difficult to adjust to the rapidly changing twenty-first century, but it's actually individuals who are mentally imprisoned by their belief system. Your ability to learn, perceive, act, and think will be more fixated in your subconscious mind the more you age, only if you allow it.

However, the capacity of your mind to transform and grow is unlimited because of the power of neuroplasticity.

Therefore, since the brain is the most important part of who you are, you need to be deliberate of what information you allow into your brain. Your ability to think and take responsibility will increase by the regular repetition of productive behavior and deep focus.

Visualizations for Your New Identity

Now that you know our minds are what we repeatedly think, act and feel you must also understand that modern science acknowledges that your brain can not tell the difference between physical action and mental visualization of the same action. You may already have a false identity of not being deeply focused. I am going to show you that you are a deeply concentrated person and before we can dive into the actual techniques proven to skyrocket focus, we must reprogram your false identity as a baseline.

For 10 minutes a day visualize your ideal deeply focused, productive, efficient and intentional self. How do you handle work obstacles that arise? How do you handle distractions? Imagine yourself as intensely, relentlessly concentrated on everything you do. Notice how you feel when you imagine yourself completing your work early and having enough time to spend pursuing your favorite hobby or being with your family.

The imagination of your future will train your brain into functioning as if you are living in your future. By focusing on the future, you are ditching your past failures, thoughts, and identity.

Identity forming visualizations are also an excellent way

to keep you on track when hit with an unnecessary distraction. Visualize how you will feel once your goal is accomplished. Through visualization, you can redirect your mind back to the current task with rejuvenated focus and willpower.

Make sure you take a few moments after waking up and before sleeping to remind yourself of your larger purpose. Why are you prioritizing a deeply focused life? Eventually, such a practice will nudge you to the direction of your goals. Let's take a step back and examine how powerful the mind can be and how feasible such a change is for any individual.

A person's state of mind has the power to determine the speed of their recovery from an illness or injury.

Individuals like Dr. Joe Dispenza have demonstrated the power of visualizations. He completely recovered from being diagnosed with indefinite paralysis from getting hit by a car while racing his bike in 1986. He chose to neglect a surgery that all the medical professionals in the country suggested that he do or else he would never walk again. Instead, he opted to experiment with healing the vertebrae of his spine through mental imaging, belief, and positive emotions. In his book 'Evolve your Brain: The Science of Changing your Mind' he said that he would spend 3 hours a day for 6.5 weeks laying in the hospital visualizing his 6 vertebrae healing from compression fractures. After that 6.5-week period, he said that his visualizations were getting easier and he "hit a sweet spot" where he could finish his visualization in 45 minutes a day. After 10.5 weeks he was back on his feet doing physical therapy and within 12 he was back to his life and started training for triathlons again. When he was healing, he told himself that if he was able to walk again, he would begin training people on how to master their mind and body connection. He continues to educate thousands of people in more than 33 countries on how we can rewire brains to be any way we want.

One of the biggest rules to unlocking the full-blown effects of visualizations is the placebo and faith effect.

The placebo effect tricks the brain into healing if you fully believe in the power of visualization and within yourself. Research has shown that when a person has faith, their brain undergoes psychological, physiological, and hormonal changes.

For example, when you consume a real painkiller or a placebo, your brain processes both in a similar fashion. When you believe something to be accurate, the chemistry of your brain transforms. If you expected to get rid of the pain, through a placebo, your brain has the power to convince your mind to believe in its healing capacity. The brain can secrete endogenous opiates, which act like painkillers produced by the body.

Thus, visualization enhances the ability of your brain to get positive results in any aspect of your physiology, brain and life.

Your new identity vision can be anything that suits your personal desires. The power of visualization only works through repetition, positive emotions and faith in the future.

You do not need any unique talents for harnessing the power of visualization. The degree of clarity in your vision, positive emotions associated with your new identity and the certainty that it will work, will empower you to choose the level of focus that you desire and can be attained through the power of neuroplasticity.

Affirmations for Your New Thoughts

Once you have a mental picture of what your new ideal reality self looks, acts and feels like now we can begin curating your new thought patterns. For most of us that is being able to deeply concentrate on the present moment in work, recreation, and family.

Reciting affirmations is the best way to create new identity thoughts that will replace your old unhelpful thoughts. They are most effective when repeated daily, with emotion and faith.

The effects of self-affirmation on our brains can be depicted through a case study conducted by researchers of the University of Michigan, UCLA, and Annenberg School for Communication.

The technology of functional magnetic resonance imaging revealed that self-affirmation has an impact on the reward centers of your brain. The pleasure centers – the ventromedial prefrontal cortex and ventral striatum - get activated through self-affirmation. These centers also get activated when you consume your favorite food or succeed in a competition.

Christopher Cascio says, "Affirmation takes advantage of our reward circuits, which can be quite powerful." He also highlighted the pain-alleviating and balancing impacts of self-affirmation in threatening situations.

It was further revealed that there is a rise in brain activity in the posterior cingulate and the prefrontal cortex of the brain. Both these regions are linked to the processing of information related to the self. According to Cascio, when there is a rise in brain activity relating to the self - negativity, pain and threatening sensations are lessened.

This study also highlights the difference in past-oriented self-affirmations and future-oriented self-affirmations. The pleasure centers of the brain received higher activity when the participants were given future based self-affirmations. The heightened emotions we feel when focusing on the positive future is what will spark the most change into our lives.

Cascio elaborates on the complications that arise in the course of behavior transformation. He says that advice can threaten the sense of self competence within people. The aim is to make people consider the validity of contrasting information offered to them. As per his theory, we need to identify neural systems that control self-affirmation so we can successfully plan intervention methods to change the brain. Future oriented self-affirmation is far more effective than education on the dangers of an individual's chosen activity. This will ensure that the intended interventions are effective in changing each individual's self-awareness and igniting reward centers of the brain.

Therefore, you must teach your brain to direct affirmations to do something you desire in the future instead of something you want to avoid. There is a difference between "I focus deeply every day" versus "I want to avoid distraction." Be intentional with your thoughts. They become words. Be intentional with your words they become your identity.

Many insanely successful people use self-affirmations to achieve whatever they want. Muhammad Ali, 1964 Heavy Weight Boxing Champion used the affirmation, "I am the greatest".

In the beginning of starting affirmations, there is an art to tricking our brains into adopting them as our own natural thoughts especially when they are goal oriented. They must be worded as a work in progress otherwise the mind will discredit them as not true. Let's say that you are climbing the corporate ladder in your company. A futile affirmation would be, "I am the CEO." Your brain will immediately discredit this thought as absurd and will impede your progress of curating your beliefs. Instead try wording your affirmation as, "I am working towards being the CEO every day". Or "I will be CEO in the near future". This is a programmable thought because your brain immediately believes it as a possibility. For emotion or mindset affirmations opt for using the present tense for the best results. Affirmations such as "I am laser focused" can be effective once some belief is established because you must be open to the possibility of diving into focus in the present.

To get the best results, you must be very specific and brief in your wording. Make sure you incorporate one emotion driving word. Thoughts trigger emotions and emotions trigger action and action triggers change. Mentioned below are some steps for creating daily affirmations:

1. Always begin with the phrase "I am." These words will help you focus your energy entirely on your identity.

2. Word your affirmations in the future tense unless they already believed as true. "I am building focus everyday" is best for someone who is not focused yet.

3. State the affirmations in the positive, for example, "I will be wildly successful," instead of "I will not

fail." Focus on what you want, not what you don't want.

4. Your affirmations should be as brief as possible and easily memorable.

5. Make use of action words that end with "ing."

6. Include emotive words which trigger a feeling. "I am pursuing the life of my wildest dreams."

7. Make yourself the center of the affirmation.

However, before we finish our list of personal affirmations, we must understand what our current thoughts and beliefs are in order to eradicate them effectively.

Replacing Beliefs Exercise

You may face problems when you try to let go of your old beliefs. Emotional, physical, and external triggers can solidify your beliefs into becoming rigid and automatic. To achieve the goal of supreme focus, you must trick your mind into ditching the old beliefs by replacing them with new ones.

You need to carry out a reprogramming exercise to transform your negative belief systems.

Take a piece of paper and fold it in half. Title the left side current beliefs and the right-side new beliefs. Keep the piece of paper in your pocket all day. As a thought arises write it down on the left-hand side. Try not to judge your thoughts and be honest with yourself as there is no right answer. After 3 days you will have a long list of thoughts. These are your current beliefs. Some are useful and some are detrimental. At the end of the last day write down your new belief that you want to replace for the belief in the corresponding left column. The new beliefs on the right-hand column are going to be your new identity affirmations.

Every morning and night repeat out loud these new beliefs. You may feel odd or silly at first, find somewhere private and take this seriously as your focus and fulfillment depends on it. For the best results, find an affirmations application on your phone or voice recording application that can record you saying your affirmations. Leave a silent pause after every affirmation to leave you room to recite it yourself. Once your list is done you can listen to yourself from a third person perspective say your new identity affirmations then repeat them as your own after each one. This is the secret method that will provide the most profound and staggering results that will compound into every area of your life, unleashing the floodgates of focus.

Subliminals

While affirmations are an extremely effective and proven method to reprogram the mind for focus another contemporary, less studied technique is on the rise. Subliminal messaging can be extremely effective in training your mind to focus. Subliminal messages are thoughts embedded in your subconscious mind from external stimuli. According to scientific research, the brain records visuals and memories that you are not consciously aware of.

Neuroscientist Bahador Bahrami, from University College London, discovered that increased activity and utilization of the brain curbs the impact of subliminal messaging. Therefore, your brain is less susceptible to being programmed when you are actively using your mind. The best results come from calming the mind, slowing the stimuli and then using a subliminal messaging soundtrack.

His work opposes psychology, which assumes that consciousness and the level of attention are directly proportional. Research has discovered that choices can be shaped by subliminal messages. But it still has not been able to determine whether these responses occur automatically or if it can be impacted by increased attention to stimuli.

Dr. Baharami's experiment concluded that the primary visual cortex of the brain is triggered by subliminal messages. The primary cortex is the first part of the brain to receive messages from the retina. The technique we are going to experiment with is auditory subliminal messaging.

The concept of subliminal brain messages is used in subliminal advertising, which is legalized in the US and might produce effective results. Bahrami speculated that advertisements are created to evoke subliminal imaging in the brain. This makes the customer crave for a specific type of product without any knowledge of the advertisement's impact on their choice.

The best way to utilize this phenomenon are specific subliminal soundtracks that are laid with voices of people saying affirmations geared towards your desired result. Usually they are also laid with isochronic tones, binaural beats, nature sounds or a blend of all three. The voices in the subliminal tracks are not noticeable which is best because it is targeting your subconscious. You may hear the voices faintly but are usually still indistinguishable. Avoid doing any complex tasks while listening to subliminal messages. Your brain is the most susceptive to programming in a relaxed state. Many people play a subliminal on repeat all night while they are sleeping however you must be careful because that is not the best for your hearing. The key is to listen to the subliminal daily and consistently while doing mundane chores, walking or relaxing. Be patient with the subliminal process, many individuals report not noticing results immediately. Keep the volume on low and always use headphones otherwise the subliminal track will not work. The best place to find subliminals in my experience is trusted specific video streaming channels. Always read the comments before listening to a subliminal to at least somewhat verify its effectiveness. Subliminals are contemporary and cutting edge however many successful people swear by their results. Start with affirmations first as they are proven and effective and then experiment with subliminals if you desire. The results are compelling and hard to ignore. I have 2 very specific video streaming channels that I use for finding focus optimizing subliminals. They have hundreds of comments from people that have tested their effectiveness over the course of years.

Gratitude Approach

We have to be grateful for what we have and who we are before we can change ourselves or strive for more. Otherwise, dissatisfaction will potentially lead to frustration, aggressiveness, insecurity, uncertainty, resentment, and emptiness. This is equivalent to failure.

The quickest and easiest way to cultivate gratitude in your life is to start a gratitude journal. This simple habit will completely change your life. You must note down at least ten things you are grateful for in your journal every day. Use a journal application on your phone that syncs with your computer or a physical one works just fine as well.

A research conducted by Christina Karns from the University of Oregon revealed the positive impact of gratitude journaling on seventeen women who were the subjects of the study. Through the regular practice of recording what you are grateful for, you can rejuvenate your emotions and brain.

When we are grateful for the goals, we have already achieved then we will have more energy and focus to tackle our next goal. Whenever you count your blessings, you are grateful for how far you have come. This channels your focus into maintaining your current state of being and eventually elevating it to achieve more success. It also builds empathy in your mind for those who are less fortunate than you. Such a reaction keeps your brain positive and rejuvenated for continuous progress. Failure to cultivate the habit of gratitude will ensure a life of unfulfillment.

Make use of the gratitude approach in your daily life by writing down 10 people, experiences, objects or aspects of yourself that you are grateful for every day.

Summary

Once you begin training your brain through affirmations, subliminals, the gratitude approach, and your new beliefs exercise, your new focused and satisfied self will emerge. You are capable of being as deeply focused as you desire at any minute. You are already innately satisfied, fulfilled, joyful, ultimately focused and productive. Never believe anyone that tells you otherwise no matter what their "qualifications" or "degrees" are. This was the first step for me when I rose above my belief of having an ADD broken brain.

Action Steps

- Write down your ideal workday of focus and new identity for your visualization exercise.
- Do the replacing beliefs exercise. Every time a negative belief arises. Write it down, and right next to it, pen down your ideal belief.
- Choose either affirmations or subliminals.
- Affirmations: Take all your new beliefs from the new beliefs exercise and record yourself, saying them with an app. Use a short pause at the end so you can repeat the affirmation while you listen to it once or twice a day for best results.
- Subliminals: Find a focus geared subliminal from a trusted source on a video streaming website. Listen to it twice a day with headphones. Make sure to read the comments first.
- At the end of every day, write down ten things that you are grateful for.

2

HABITS - AUTOMATING YOUR LIFE FOR SUCCESS

Successful people are defined through all the micro habits they mentally and physically perform. At any given stage in your life, there is a set of activities that you repeat so often that they become automatic and second nature to you. Everything - from how you wake up and dress for work to how you like to eat dinner - falls into the category of a habit. You may think that your habits don't have too much of a bearing on your ability to work deeply, but you are mistaken. Your habits are born out of the environment you live in at home and work. They started as a series of decisions that you made on a day-to-day basis and turned into unconscious habits. All decision making is a deliberative process, in which your brain consciously and subconsciously analyses the pros and cons of a certain choice, based on many factors that constitute your environment. Therefore, even the smallest decisions can compound and chip away at the cognitive power of your brain over the course of your work day. The job of habits is to minimize cognitive power used. One of the best life hacks is learning how to utilize and automate habits to enhance our focus.

Neuroscientific studies show that when a habit is

created, the basal ganglia, which is responsible for decision-making, takes over the choice of what the next motor or perceptual decision will be. The basal ganglia along with the frontal cortex, and lateral intraparietal area are hugely responsible for reducing the amount of conscious thinking that goes into each decision. This is to free up the 'thinking capacity' of the brain so that it can be used for more important decisions that need intense deliberation. The human mind does not have a limitless capacity to think in between resting states, and it slowly exhausts itself through the day through decisions. The smaller decisions that you make later in the day then appear more complex to you, inducing frustration and exhaustion of mental energy. We will eventually discuss how to increase our thresholds of exhaustion, and how to better manage our cognitive capacity by harnessing neuroplasticity in chapters nine and ten. To combat this our brains, enter this state called the default mode network. This is the energy saving autopilot state that we enter while doing cognitively easy and familiar tasks. It is triggered when we begin to think intently on information that is not the task at hand while doing a mundane task such as laundry. The default mode network can be used for solving problems, increasing self-awareness or for harboring a habit of distraction. This autopilot mode is pivotal to maintaining our cognitive energy levels as long as we avoid the habit of multitasking. We must learn how to harness the default mode network or we will use it to be distracted.

You may be wondering how much space these decisions occupy in the decision-making process, given their trivial and perceived inconsequential nature. Behavioral studies done in 2014 tell us that up to 40% of the average adult schedule is just habits. This implies that almost half the activities that you do through the day are run on autopilot. Why not use this auto pilot system to transform normally challenging tasks such as deep concentration into easy habits that don't waste your brain's energy. One of the best ways to optimize the use of mental capacity is to carefully study your routine and make the most low-level decisions that you have to make in a day as automatic as possible. This is not very complicated, since most individuals follow a natural and specific routine every day. Mundane activities like getting dressed, eating, exercising, paying bills, stocking the kitchen, and laundry becomeF less emotionally draining if they are planned in advance, done routinely, and in clusters. Optimizing your routine to drain less of your energy is essential and we will cover that more later in the book.

The system that regulates your decisions when you are not carrying out automated habits is often called self-control or willpower. Willpower is the mental energy meter of your decision making and self-regulating system. Many successful experts in focus express our limited ability to make quality decisions over the course of the day.

Research conducted by the University of Minnesota and Florida State University conclude our mental energy is depleted when making decisions. They had two groups of students scan through a course catalog, one group had to choose courses that lined up with their required credits and the other group just scanned the catalog. After both groups were given a choice, if they wanted to study for 15 minutes immediately after for an exam that the researchers would give out later or if they wanted to relax. The catch is all participants were given the option to scan magazines or play a video game with that 15 minutes instead. The students who made decisions, choosing the courses they wanted, gave up studying after 8.5 minutes on average. Students who didn't make decisions spent roughly 11.5 minutes studying. The same team ran a couple other studies all concluding that the size or importance of the decision is irrelevant when judging the energy consumption. It was the amount of decisions that gave the students diminishing returns on their ability to regulate themselves. This concludes that the more trivial decisions we make, the more havoc we wreak on our ability to control ourselves.

However, before you write off willpower as a finite resource, I must include a relatively new cutting-edge study done by Stanford University Ph.D. researcher Veronika Job. She is exposing the links between perceived willpower and actual willpower reserves. She conducted a study in 2010 where subjects who believed their willpower was infinite did not show signs of depletion after using self-control. While the subjects that viewed willpower as limited showed signs of exhaustion after using self-control. A second part of that study, researchers manipulated and primed the individuals by administering subtly biased questionnaires before they took the test. The Individuals who were led to believe that willpower was finite showed signs of "ego depletion", another name for self-control depletion. While the volunteers who were led to believe that willpower was limitless didn't show signs of ego depletion.

It is important that we understand that our brains have a limited amount of energy the same way our bodies do. However, we must understand even deeper that we rarely ever reach that max threshold. Our brains are much more resilient than we are led to believe. All we have to do is believe that our willpower is unlimited.

Albeit, even with an unlimited willpower we must use our decision making and self-regulating resources effectively for maximum work output. To save mental energy we must understand what initiates a habit in the first place. Then we can understand how to exploit this autopilot system in our favor.

Understanding Triggers

To gain more control over your automatic habits, it is important to have a thorough understanding of your habit triggers. What constitutes a habit trigger? The Society for Personality and Social Psychology says that 'habits emerge through associative learning.' Basically, a habit is an association between stimuli and responses. When you learn an activity, it activates a large set of neural circuits. The motor and premotor regions of the neocortex, the cerebellum, the dorsal striatum and the basal ganglia. The brain does not usually create urges to do activities ad hoc; it is set off by many associative and contextual factors. Anything that the mind associates with the automatic urge to do a regular activity can be called a habit trigger. Habit triggers are responsible for kick-starting the entire mental-physical process through which a habit is completed. Habit triggers become stronger through repetition creating a stronger neuron synapse which is the scientific name for getting more comfortable in a certain thought or activity. Every time the trigger actually precedes the habit, its association with the habit becomes increasingly stronger and not easily breakable. Hence the saying, an old dog can't learn new tricks. That is ultimately not true due to neuroplasticity however it can require more effort to rewire strong neural synapses built up over lifetimes.

There is a lot of scientific work on the associative

relationship between a habit and a stimulus. In neuroscience, it is called Hebbian learning which was introduced by Canadian Neuropsychologist Donald Hebb, in his book "The Organization of Behavior" in 1949. The Hebbian theory tries to explain this kind of associative learning. It says that when a group of cells is activated simultaneously in the brain, there is an increase in the synaptic strength between them. The more those cells are activated together, the stronger the brain's memory of that simultaneousness activation is, and therefore, the stronger the trigger or thought pattern is. The theory is often popularly summarized as 'neurons that fire together wire together.' In simpler words, the association between a trigger and a habit can be made stronger through performing it more often until you're running on energy saving autopilot mode. When your habits have strong associations with their triggers, then the habits must be prevented by removing or avoiding those triggers entirely. Trying to resist performing a habit when the triggering stimulus is present will deplete your mental resources unnecessarily and most often result in failure. Our goal is to save all of our cognitive energy for our deep state focusing sessions.

Replacing Habit Triggers

Now that you have a basic understanding of what triggers are, you can use them to automate your life and conserve energy. Anything in your environment can be a potential habit-trigger or can be transformed into one. By associating certain habits with certain pre-existing events, a certain time of day, a certain location, a certain individual, or a certain object that you regularly encounter, you can turn your routine into an effortless and mechanical task. These triggers need to be fairly consistent and frequent but also time-bound. Have triggers that happen at approximately the same time every day if possible. The triggers should not require any effort on your part for them to happen for them to work the best. They will not be avoidable if you're trying to build a good habit. The point of a trigger is that there has to be as little space as possible to manipulate it. A great example of a habit trigger is this app that you can set to make a vibration on your phone at regular intervals. Then you associate the specific tone or vibration with a behavior that you want to do such as standing up straight instead of slouching. This habit takes a constant reminder so frequent triggers like this are useful. However, this specific example is not useful during times of a day that you need to focus. More examples of triggers are, the same time blocked work schedule, an isochronic tone track, or a quick cardio session. If you have a goal of drinking a gallon of water a day then keeping a gallon with you will be the perfect trigger. The options are endless and only limited by your creativity. You only have to put conscious work on strengthening the association of the activity you have with the trigger, rather than orchestrating a routine or making decisions.

Habit Chunking

Another way to replace or create new habits is habit chunking. The most fundamental step towards change is the careful study of your routine. It is not enough to simply know your general motor and perceptual actions throughout the day. You want to have a sense of the specific things in the routine that you would like to change, as well as a knowledge of the larger habit goal you want to attain by changing your routine. The changes that you would like to make in your routine consist of a combination of good habits to make life easier and reducing bad habits that create resistance.

Fundamentally, habit chunking is the technique of adding or stacking a new habit that you want to develop on top of a pre-existing habit exclusively. This technique exploits the associative learning patterns of the brain that have been made stronger through many years of repetition. The brain is both familiar with and friendly to these patterns because they have emerged from the lifelong process of a neuroscientific phenomenon known as synaptic pruning. As the information and behaviors we learn become more complex we remove connections that no longer serve us and keep only the most efficient functioning neuron synapses. As an infant, your brain becomes accustomed to repetitive activities, and therefore the connections between your neurons, called synapses, are not strong in any particular direction. As you grow and your brain starts to identify recurring activities, it prunes away the unused synapses and reallocates that energy to strengthening frequently used synaptic patterns. This process is associated with skill development. For example, if you have a cup of coffee in the morning every day for many years, that is a well-established synaptic connection that is connected to the time of day and the activity of waking up. If you are trying to incorporate a new habit into your routine, instead of carving out an entirely new path for it, stack it on top of the existing habit of drinking coffee. Every time you finish your morning coffee, tackle your hardest problem first for an hour. Keep these behaviors exclusive to each other or else the trigger will not work. The key is to only reward yourself with the dopamine inducing coffee when you are building this new discipline habit. The coffee will help build a Pavlovian conditioning association between coffee and deep focus. Similar to when Pavlov rang the bell and the dog salivated. Another example is having a deep focus desk, and chair. Have a separate desk and chair (or at least chair) that you only ever sit in when doing your most important deep work. This tactic is especially helpful for those who work at home or find themselves using the same space for recreation and work. The chair and desk can be substituted for a specific deep concentration associated cafe work space. Once you sit in this dedicated deep focus space you get straight to your most challenging task at hand first in the morning and pair with your favorite coffee for twice the habit conditioning effects.

You are more likely to sustain an activity and transform it into a habit if you can do it without breaking the momentum of the routine that you are accustomed to. You can use this simple technique as a building block for widening the network of associated behaviors that you want to implement in your life.

Habit Substitution

Habit substitution is an especially helpful technique for individuals with an accidentally unproductive routine because it has the dual benefit of getting rid of an older habit while developing a new easier one. It works with the same process of association, as elaborated in the previous section. However, instead of identifying a pattern and adding an activity, you identify the negative pattern and replace the pre-existing habit with the new habit that you want to develop. Habit substitution is recommended for people who are trying to break challenging and undesired habits because replacing a bad habit is easier than simply trying to stop or avoid the temptation. Habit chunking is more effective for starting a new unrelated good habit. For example, if you tend to scroll through social media on your lunch break then try sitting with several coworkers instead who are having an active conversation. The conversation of the coworkers will give you that sense of social entertainment that you are seeking, and as a plus you can always ask them what the latest interesting stories are.

The first step to habit substitution is to identify whether the habit is triggered by a location, time or an event. Next is to find a way to avoid coming across that trigger altogether. Such as walking to the park on your lunch break. This will prevent you from looking at your phone and give you some much needed time to clear your thoughts before the next deep focus session. With the trigger gone, you will find it easier to not scroll idly to conserve mental energy for work. If you are struggling with going to the gym after work, try avoiding going home at all. After work head straight to the gym and sit in the parking lot with your gym clothes always loaded in the car. The temptation to stay home will be gone and you are much less likely to drive back home after sitting in the gym parking lot for a minute. If you have a habit of grabbing an alcoholic beverage after a hard day of work then remove the alcohol from the house. You can always go grab some if you want some but that extra barrier will often deter us. Without habit substitution removing these habits on your own requires a tremendous amount of precious energy that could be used for focusing. This is like telling you not to think about pink elephants. Of course, you start to think about pink elephants because it was mentioned. If I tell you to think of red zebras when my goal is to get you to avoid thinking about pink elephants then we completely avoid the problem all together.

"Don't Break the Chain" – Habit Tracking

Jerry Seinfeld, one of the highest-selling and most successful comedians of the last decade, reportedly followed an innovative system to pressurize him to keep writing every day, even with an incredibly busy schedule. He would take a large wall calendar and hang it on a wall that was visible and unavoidable. Each day when he finished his writing, he would cross out the corresponding date on the calendar with a big red X. After only a few days of working regularly, a chain of red X's would start forming on his wall calendar. By being able to visualize the consistency of his writing habit, he would get motivated to simply not break the chain. Seinfeld himself insists on the importance of not skipping any days since even one break in the chain can trigger a series of skips. He offered this as advice to a young comedian who once met him on a comedy tour, but this technique is relevant to any kind of habit that you want to undergo.

This technique works in incremental, daily action synergistically with the compound effect. A large, abstract goal like 'write more often' is turned into a simple, everyday task that can be crossed off on a calendar such as write for 1 hour a day. The cumulative satisfaction of doing the task every day will be more visible to you. It is also extremely effective for skill-building. By repeating the task every day, you can gain expertise quickly and reduce the amount of energy you have to expend in finishing it for the future. This compounded effect of a little work done every day has proven to be a better strategy than overworking yourself for short bursts of time and with irregular frequency, that leads to premature burnout.

Scheduling Rewards

Another effective conditioning technique for training ourselves to stick with consistency is to give ourselves mini and large rewards for certain tasks completed. Aim to reward yourself for consistent behavior on a weekly and monthly basis depending on the skill. This also creates an incentive for you to finish your tasks with regularity while not making your routine feel too dull. These rewards can be small ones – an outing to the movie theatre, lunch with an old friend, pursuing a loved hobby, or grabbing a fancy cappuccino. You need to schedule these small rewards at least every week as an incentive and motivation to complete small goals. You can also schedule bigger rewards for yourself, such as mini weekend vacations, spa trips, or visiting a favorite restaurant. These mini-rewards and big-rewards are shown to have incredible effects on the morale of a person and can make all these techniques easy to follow.

Remember that you already live in a culture where rewards are constantly encouraged and the basic idea of a reward is skewed. You are surrounded by advertisements that try to manipulate you into buying products and services. Rewards, such as a big purchase of expensive shoes instead of paying off a long-standing loan, are counter-productive to your long-term concentration. The stress of making your financial situation worse will chip away at your mental energy and focus. Effective rewarding is more complex than you may assume. This is why even highly motivated people sometimes bypass the reward technique, resulting in premature burnout, loss of motivation, fatigue, a compromised personal life, and poor health. A researcher at Harvard found that progress is perceived by people as the best reward. The satisfaction of having done a full day of work is its own reward, and nothing else that you do will match that level of satisfaction. To make the most of this progress-driven reward feeling, you can try the following things.

Break down every major goal into mini steps – the smaller and simpler the steps, the better. Put the big picture aside, and focus on the simple things you need to do every day to achieve a larger goal.

Divert your focus away from 'completion' towards things done right. There is a subtle difference between the two, to do a pre-decided task to the best of your ability makes the victory so much sweeter and fulfilling.

Make your rewards as healthy as you possibly can. Consider revising rewarding yourself with a night of drunken partying as a prize for meeting your productivity goals. A night out with friends can do wonders for your morale. However, when coupled with excessive drinking your productivity will tank and possibly cause more stress at work than needed. Carefully weigh the pros and cons of these decisions to find the best choice for your focus. Instead, opt for things like learning a relaxing new skill, home/workplace makeovers, taking a fitness class, card games with friends etc. The more you can involve your loved ones, the better. This system of work and reward will create a remarkably healthy cycle in your life.

Summary

The goal is to obtain AI level subconscious productive habits for the tasks that give you the highest quality life experience so that the new and challenging tasks will be learned easier. Carefully examine your current habits and triggers. Identify which ones hinder or boost your concentration and make adjustments appropriately.

Action Steps

- Write down your current habits and potential triggers.
- Write down your ideal new habits along with new triggers.
- Pair good habits with good food, coffee, or other fun activities and only do those activities with those good habits.
- Find clever ways to avoid locations, certain times and events that trigger poor habits by replacing them with a new healthier habit.
- Write down ideas for small and large goal rewards.
- Download a habit-tracking app or keep a separate calendar and red marker for each positive habit.

3

DISTRACTIONS - THE SILENT KILLER OF DREAMS

"He who wants the rose must respect the thorn"

PERSIAN PROVERB

What was once the main survival technique in the prehistoric era has now replaced the tyrannosaurus rex as the deadliest predator. To understand distractions, we have to scientifically study why our brains tend to look for ways to avoid doing the things it's supposed to do. If we go back to our ancestors, and the development of our brains, what we find is that our brains learned to focus on multiple stimuli at once as an evolutionary tactic to keep us alive. Since evolution was all about survival of the fittest, humans had to develop a way to look for things in the environment that automatically shift our concentration to help increase our chances of noticing anything threatening. We literally needed our brain to scan the environment around us and to constantly be on edge for any usual noise or movement. This meant that if our ancestors were cooking or farming, they had to find a way to ensure that their job didn't completely grab their entire attention, so their brains evolved to be on the lookout for distractions. Since the game of survival has now changed, you have to produce more value by producing more mental output in fewer hours. This can be a bit confusing for us because our brains are hardwired to look for distractions, and what we're trying to do is to have unwavering focus. Instinctually, having unwavering focus where you lose yourself in your work is unnatural but can be mastered.

Many knowledge workers view distractions as a constant struggle to fight against. However, distractions are not something we necessarily fight off. Being in a constant state of resisting and fighting urges will leave our minds battered like our bodies would be after a day at battle. Instead we must view distractions as a necessary evil that can be sidestepped most of the time and utilized to our advantage the rest of the time. Many knowledge workers go hour after hour resisting the urge to browse the internet during work hours. That is a waste of energy that can be avoided. Perhaps we are getting some work done at home and our children or family needs our attention for a moment. If your family respects your boundaries then they will understand the value of your focus and only interject when it is highly important or time sensitive. We must utilize these moments of distraction to aid us instead of harm us.

We must first study how our brains focus on tasks and how much energy it takes for us to focus, to get a clearer idea of how to deal with this dilemma. Researchers have found that how we focus is not through an uninterrupted stream, but through bursts of high intensity focus.

This helps us in placing distractions in scientific analysis, so you can study your behavior and have some control over it to change the choices that your brain makes. Your brain scans the environment (every four seconds according to scientific studies) to find out if there are any threats that require your attention, then it goes back to what needs your attention. The most surefire way to prevent yourself from being drawn into the other stimuli is by preventing yourself from seeing it all together. Many writers will seek seclusion in a mountain cabin or fill their ethernet port with glue to avoid the temptations of novelty. For many of us a more practical solution is a website blocker built into our browser. That way we can still work with the internet but avoid pleasurable internet browsing.

This is the most useful technique for fighting the distraction built into our DNA. Remove the 'predator' from entering our field of vision and focus deeper on hunting or gathering.

While our attention span may have been more cohesive earlier, with the rapid spread of information, technology, and entertainment, our attention span has been trained to be more fragmented and scattered while our need to focus for longer periods of time is increasing every year. We seek novel stimuli and immediate gratification ferociously as a society. News stories get shorter and shorter slowly every year. We scan through pictures on social media faster and faster every year. We want short and easily consumable pieces that require no effort but great reward for the reward centers of the brain. If an article is too long, we'll just dump it and move on to something else that is trying to grab our attention. With the advent of shorter and shorter articles, blog posts, and social media stories, we are always on the lookout for something that can distract us better by being more interesting. Scientific research can attest to this as a proven fact – in 2004, our attention span used to be 3 minutes and 5 seconds, and in 2016 it moved to 40 seconds, according to Gloria Mark of the University of

California Irvine, who studies digital distraction.

However, we are not helpless when it comes to tackling this society wide attention span Armageddon. At a single point in time, there are thousands of things that are fighting to get our attention, and our mind thinks that they are all equivalently important. We must learn to prioritize.

First and foremost, we have to take a moment to understand different forms of distractions in order to come up with a distraction action plan.

Internal Distractions

Internal distractions are about your own inner desires. There are three types of internal distractions:

1. Pleasure Based: Your brain breaks your attention span whenever you get bored with what you're doing, and instead looks for new things that can give you pleasure. Example, watching tv shows instead of listening to or reading a book on the same topic.

2. Cognitive Ease Based: Paying attention for a long period to only one task or thought takes a lot of energy, and our brain tends to distract us, easing the mental burden. Example, hearing your phone buzz and halting your reading of this book.

3. Avoiding Threats Based: As I stated earlier, our brain breaks our attention span every few seconds to search for stimuli that might cause us harm. Example, our boss yelling at us or giving out a write up.

External Distractions

These are distractions that exist beyond your own needs and are a part of the external environment that you occupy. These external factors demand our attention and, therefore, end up distracting us from what we're supposed to do. Example, our significant other asking us what we want for dinner.

Technology is a Tool

Technology can be considered to be inherently distracting because it can be such a constant stream of novelty. It's challenging to avoid when compared to a less stimulating activity such as a walk or curling up with a good book. But there is still a level of choice that we exercise when it comes to getting distracted by technology. It's not technology as a whole that we should blame. We must take some individual responsibility to study how we use technology to make ourselves distracted.

Let's look at the historical relationship between past technology and how society felt about its inception. The invention of the alphabet was not warmly welcomed by philosophers in Ancient Greece. For Socrates the problem with external information storage is, it was perceived to distract us by replacing our memory recall. The invention of the alphabet, according to him, meant that it would be easier for us to be distracted by words. That eventually, it would reduce our ability to memorize since writing would replace our brain as a way of storing information. They had strong roots in learning by application instead of theories. Much of this still stands true. However, as we know the alphabet overall plays a huge success in our global economy and suggesting otherwise is preposterous. We can learn from this incorrect judgement of cutting-edge technology. Most technological advances are a double edge sword. They are overwhelmingly positive; however, many individuals get eaten alive by the few negatives.

Our brains can only process a certain amount of information effectively at a time until we start experiencing diminishing returns. We process so much information daily that we don't remember the majority of it. The rest of it isn't appreciated the same as if we consumed stimuli slower and more deliberate. There is a beautiful art to practicing a more intentional life. From condensing our physical possessions, to being more present in the moment and aware of our thoughts, there is much to gain from living a life free of distracting thoughts and possessions.

If the articles or reports you read make you react emotionally, then it's bound to lead to mental fatigue. The best thing to do is to avoid the news and social media friends that post anxiety inducing content. They suck the energy out of you and hinder your concentration. We will discuss more of the worst distractions and how to avoid them in Chapter 9, 'Mental Energy Management'.

A simple solution is to approach technology like the Amish. There is a cultural myth that says that the Amish completely avoid technology, it's far from true – in reality, some are quite pro-technology, but only technology that can makes their lives happier. Many people think that they 'throw the baby out with the bathwater' as far as technology is concerned. The truth is many Amish have an intentional method to approaching technology. They study technology critically by first removing it completely, and slowly adding it back after carefully reviewing the positives and negatives. If the benefits outweigh the negatives, then it's allowed back in; otherwise, it's thrown out. Any technology that disrupts the community or has an obsessive impact on the human mind is eliminated. For example, the Amish aren't allowed to own cars because they noticed that car owners would increasingly desert the community to partake in individualist activities such as sightseeing or picnics. The Amish view the absence of cars as a way to bring a family and community closer together. Any technology that distracts them from their core values of community, hospitality, connection, faith, morale, fulfillment and happiness is perceived as a hindrance. Obviously, I am not promoting that you sell all your possessions and begin farming on a homestead. We must use the methodology of the Amish to eliminate or add specific technology into our lives. For example, social media is a fantastic way to connect with old friends. There are social groups for just about any topic that can help us learn and grow. Connecting with like-minded people is very important. However, scrolling through your feed is usually not an activity that boosts your energy and focus. Instead of deleting all your social media accounts, simply installing a news feed blocker on your browser or an app that blocks social media during work hours is far more practical. Analyze and be ruthless with every technology in your life for the best results.

Multitasking

Certain tasks are ingrained into the neural structure of our brain so that we can do them intuitively with minimal attention and effort. While some tasks require us to focus entirely on what we're doing, others can be done with less attention.

When it comes to tasks in our knowledge careers that require us to think and pay attention to them, multitasking ends up harming our focus. Multitasking not only destroys your productivity but it also trains your brain to be in a state of distraction. For example, writing an email while at the same time trying to help a coworker. Coupling tasks together makes your cognitive resources fragmented hindering your ability to concentrate on either task. You must be intentional in how you train your brain to behave.

What you're doing is just training your brain to be bad at two tasks, which can lead to brain damage. Here's why:

- A study from the University of Sussex compared the brain structure of people who interacted with two different media devices – watching TV and texting. What they found was that those who multitasked between the two had less brain density in their anterior cingulate cortex, which is the region responsible for emotional control and empathy.

- According to Earl Miller, a neuroscientist at MIT, each time we switch between tasks, it requires energy that our brain loses. So, when you stop working deep and start replying to an email, you are losing energy, therefore, mental efficiency and performance.

- Researchers at the University of London found that those who multitasked regularly experienced a drop in IQ points.

- Multitasking also kills creativity since complete extended focus towards a task will allow you to think innovatively.

- Multitasking also hurts your decision-making skills because when you constantly switch between tasks, it leads to decision fatigue.

What's even worse than trying to multitask between two mundane tasks is trying to do two new tasks at the same time. Your brain does not do two tasks at the same time ever – it does them in a sequence. So, when you do two things like watch TV and read articles on your phone at the same time, it damages your ability to focus which can potentially lead to a less efficient brain structure long term. Neuroplasticity can work in our favor or against us. It may seem that your brain doesn't get too tired when doing two tasks that you are comfortable with at the same time. However, this is a habit that will suck the rest of your more important habits dry.

Task switching also has a detrimental effect on our focus. When you jump from one task to another, your brain takes some time to get acquainted with the new task. Your focus will stay on the last task especially if it was not completed before moving on to the new task. Attention residue is the proper term that was coined by business professor Dr. Sophie Leroy who studied the impact of performing multiple tasks sequentially in her 2009 paper. Of course, task switching cannot be avoided in a daily work schedule but unnecessary task switching must be eliminated. Whenever possible finish the current task at hand before moving on to the next and never try to do two tasks at the same time. This goes for work and your personal life. Don't be too literal with this advice because checking on your laundry while cooking at the end of the day can be helpful in saving time. However, having 20 tabs open on your internet browser that are related to multiple projects is a recipe for mental fatigue. Instead of responding to an email every time it arrives, schedule a time when you can respond to 10 of the most important emails.

Goal Work vs. Maintenance Work

There are two types of work that we conduct during our daily work days. Goal work is work that gets us closer to our ultimate happiness and fulfilment in life. Maintenance work is work that has to be done to sustain a specific job such as emails, and meetings but don't get us closer to our goals as quickly. Sometimes work that appears and "feels" productive is just an insidious distraction in disguise. At any given moment, many people have 30 tabs open, from emails to articles, this might give us the illusion of being busy, but in reality, we are just distracting ourselves, unable to focus on the work we're supposed to do.

Sort each daily work task based on what gets you closer to your goal or work that sustains your job. When it comes to a choice between checking your email and writing a report for your boss, the answer is simple – you want to focus completely on writing the report. But, instead, we tend to do maintenance work like checking our email constantly, with constant trips to the water cooler pretending that we are working, when all we're doing is distracting ourselves.

The best time to complete goal work is during the early mornings or late nights, whichever you find you have the most energy from your day. For most people it is the early mornings between 3am-7am. I have learned to become very fond of waking up at 3:30am. The first few weeks were brutal, however I learned to love the solitude. I reward myself with coffee when I wakeup this early and begin diving into writing. I have no temptation to be distracted because the only reason I put myself through the discomfort of waking up early is to tackle my biggest task. My ability to work efficiently without distraction is tenfold because of my conditioned association between 3:30 and hustling. Not everyone functions like me, choose a time that works for your personal schedule. Mozart was famous for working early in the morning and late into the nights often only getting 4-6 hours of sleep. He was recorded stating, "When I am … completely myself, entirely alone … or during the night when I cannot sleep, it is on such occasions that my ideas flow best and most abundantly. Whence and how these ideas come I know not nor can I force them."

Summary

Eliminating distractions from the inside out, will have a profound impact on your career and life. Technology is a tool that is best used for progressing towards your goals. However, all the tools are not created equal. We must examine the usefulness against the possible negatives before deciding if the specific technology is allowed into our life. Finally, use a ratio of 70-30 for goal-oriented work and maintenance-oriented work. This will boost your work output, unlock more free time, and skyrocket your satisfaction.

Action Steps

- Identify what activities distract you the most. Write them down. Next write down a pros and cons list for each activity and decide if you want to eliminate it from your life or limit it to once a week. Learn to prioritize what is most important to you in life - social time, personal beliefs, exercise, etc., and eliminate the rest.
- Download an app that will block time-wasting apps from your phone for at least evenings, mornings, and deep focus blocks.
- Turn off all notifications on your phone and desktop except for the important ones.
- Turn your phone to do not disturb.
- Leave your phone in the other room while focusing deeply.
- Install a website blocker on your internet browser on your work computer.
- Eliminate multitasking from your personal and work life.

4

OPTIMIZE YOUR WORKSPACE FOR PEAK PERFORMANCE

"Truth is ever to be found in simplicity, and not in the multiplicity and confusion of things."

ISAAC NEWTON

Less is More

We are the product of our environment. In order to build an intentional lifestyle around focus and your deepest values in life we must be intentional about the workspaces we allow into our lives as well. Your environment is your workspace and personal home along with all the objects that surround you. Optimizing our workspace is more than just organization, it is being deliberate with what gives us happiness and progressing towards our goals. Consciously curating our environment will help to induce a calm and organized brain to help you unlock new levels of concentration. A Princeton study shows that surrounding yourself with a lot of clutter is the quickest way to having a chaotic schedule which is unproductive and stress-inducing. The distraction of clutter can often lead to an inability to process information because it is fed with excessive visual stimuli. Decluttering your workspace is a gateway to decluttering your brain. While optimizing your workspace, always remember the golden rule – less is more.

To understand why decluttering is important, you first need to understand how clutter functions as a distraction and why it can be dangerous to your journey of attaining masterful focus. In a room full of things, while you may be consciously trying to focus on the task at hand, your brain is unconsciously aware of the physical presence of all the other objects. Visual information from possessions around you is fed to your brain, and this can wear down and exhaust you. For example, when sitting down to study for an important exam in college, you want to be in a fresh, clean space. If you sit next to a big pile of laundry, you will constantly be distracted by the need to do the laundry, even though studying for that exam is more important. This will make concentration more challenging.

The Minimalism of Steve Jobs

A minimalistic approach to the workspace is espoused by some of our generation's greatest minds. Steve Jobs, the great entrepreneur, and past CEO of one of the biggest companies in the world, was a minimalist in his work life and vision for the future of technology. He would wear the same outfit every day to shift his focus from what to wear to the major daily decisions of a CEO. One of his first houses in Woodside, CA, had almost no furniture, except for what was necessary. A lamp, a mattress, and a card table. This also meant that much thought went into each item that was present in his workspace. He was also an incredibly goal-oriented person, trying to always eliminate tasks and processes that weren't contributing to his larger goal. This lack of physical attachments and material possessions is not just a philosophy for monks and ascetics; it can become a very effective way of life for people who want to live intentional lives.

Follow a similar approach to your workspace. Carefully study every item that you have around you, and think about how much it contributes to your work or your happiness. If you cannot think of any essential reasons why you need an object, remove it from your workspace or life without hesitation. You can consider donating items that have not lost their value but are no longer useful to you. Ryan Nicodemus, one half of the duo called The Minimalists, who preaches minimalism and how to implement it, recommends an interesting technique. He says that you want to put all objects you own in one specific place, packed boxes or in a closet. Only remove the objects that you need one at a time as your need for them arises. If a month/year of living without the rest of those objects does not make work harder for you, get rid of them. This heavy scrutiny is really important to transform your workspace into a smooth assemblage of essential objects that help you organize your life and work.

There is a vast range of organizational equipment that you can use to replace obsolete and space-consuming setups. Smart furniture, easy-access shelves, lockable drawers, easy chairs, and many others are intelligent alternatives to traditional, non-utilitarian interiors. The point of a minimalistic workspace is not to let things accumulate around you. We want to motivate ourselves to keep our space clean and free of possessions. Once you can incorporate this level of the organization into your physical space, it will also filter into your mental space.

Clearing Digital Clutter

Beyond the physical aspect of decluttering lies the digital aspect. Since everything on the Internet is so easy to access, many people don't believe in hoarding offline files, records, and archives. Consider backing up all your information digitally on the cloud to reduce clutter on your phone and computer. Next, we need to streamline our workflow by minimizing our phone and computer interfaces. Start by deleting non-frequently used apps from your phone. For your work computer you must minimize the number of desktop icons on your personal computer, and uninstall programs that you do not directly use for work. You will also have to organize the way information reaches you. Use 'do not disturb' settings, reduce notifications, and block all distractions.

Organizing Emails

A full, unorganized email inbox can be the death of your workflow. Setting up a process to automate how your emails are organized will save you tremendous amounts of time in the future. What you don't want to be doing is organizing your email too much every day. You want a system in place to deal with new emails and not waste time individually tackling each one unless it doesn't fit into your filing system guidelines.

Use the FAST system – File, Assign to someone, Store/Scan, Trash. This is an elaborate system that speeds up the rate at which you process incoming emails. When you get an email that needs to be reviewed later you can file into folders separated by projects or clients. Use automated labels to sign the importance of an email as it comes in. Set your bosses email address or an important client as a high priority label with a bright color to help it stand out when it comes in. You can also set up emails to auto assign to folders that are separated by importance or due date. If it is a task that has to be delegated to someone else then send it to them on the spot. If you don't have that email already automated to enter its appropriate folder and with a priority level label then set it up as it arrives. Next if you need to store an email or embedded file from an email on the cloud do it. If this email has no value whatsoever either delete the email. If it's a recurring email silence from a specific email address then unsubscribe or block the address to prevent future tasks. By knowing what to do with every type of email, you will not spend hours being indecisive and unproductive. Clearing and filtering out your inbox is a task best tackled during the mid and last part of the work day.

Lighting and Temperature

Now that you know what not to have in your workspace, you can begin to think about what you do want in it, and how you can make a new workspace assist you. The first aspect is lighting. Full-spectrum lights and lights that mimic natural lighting are always preferred over incandescent or fluorescent light. The Springbrook center for autism and behavioral health has conducted studies into the impact of light as a sensory input on children with autism, or overly excited nervous systems. They have found that children focus better in full-spectrum lighting because the process of sensory integration, or processing information, is much easier in bright white full spectrum lights. Such lights are available as bulbs and lamps, but there is no alternative for real solar light. If it is possible, your workspace should be next to a window that allows light. If your desk is not near a window like the rest of us then simply replacing your work lamp bulb with a full spectrum bulb and taking a walk during a break on a sunny day is adequate. However, when performing creative work researchers from Germany demonstrated that it is recommended to work with dimmer, more ambient lighting that will soothe your brain and help ideas flow. Anna Steidle of the University of Stuttgart and Lioba Werth of the University of Hohenheim conducted 6 experiments which provide evidence for their thesis and are explained in the Journal of Environment Psychology that dim lighting, "elicits a feeling of freedom, self-determination and reduced inhibition".

Windows with an open view may also produce feelings of freedom which spark creativity. If a window is not realistic in your office, put pictures in your workspace that are mentally rejuvenating to look at for in between focus blocks. These can be beautiful nature scenes, photos of a vacation, photos of your loved ones or anything that is personally meaningful to you. The emotional aspect of creating a workspace is as important as the physical aspect.

Adjust the temperature in your office optimal for work. A study conducted by researchers from the University of Chicago studied the impact of work space temperature and productivity levels using data from factories in India. The research suggests that productivity drops by 4% per degree when temperatures are above 80 degrees Fahrenheit in factories of manual labor. Human alertness is at its peak at a temperature slightly colder than room temperature for most individuals, but not so cold that it becomes uncomfortable. Warmer temperatures are generally discouraged as they can sap energy from the body and make you lethargic. Test a temperature that works for you in your work environment. The majority of us have no control over the temperature of our office but we can always dress light and bring layers to our work.

Coworkers and Bosses

Your life will be much easier once you get your coworkers, boss or employees to understand the importance of goal-oriented work without distraction. There is a perfect goal to maintenance work balance to maintain, and you must explain to them the difference between the two. Come up with a healthy ratio, tracking the minimum number of hours of maintenance work and presenting your case for more goal-oriented work to your boss. This might go without saying but present the information to your boss as a way to boost the productivity for the company as a whole. You are trying to work harder and deeper by cutting down unnecessary maintenance work and distractions. While goals are what show tangible progress, maintenance is what helps keep your coworkers in the loop and boosts the illusion of productivity with your peers. An ideal work-maintenance ratio is 70:30. At least 70% of our time needs to be spent on company goal-oriented work. You must track the number of hours in your day that is devoted to your goals and maintenance work, and show it to your boss, coworkers or employees to make them understand the importance of working deeply. Sometimes it can feel like the company you work for perceives immediately responding to an email as "working harder", giving the illusion of being more productive. When in reality instead of emailing back you could be fine tuning that major project or obtaining that new client. This is the key to companywide process-based efficiency. This false perception of productivity is a virus that is plaguing the modern-day workforce. Perception is important to maintaining a career but everyone needs to understand the costs.

Inform them of your new twice a day email management schedule to see if it is viable to implement. Preferably you will answer emails in the late morning or mid-day after doing a few hours of deep work along with a time right before your work day ends so you know what to work on the following morning. An autoresponder helps tremendously for deterring coworkers and will reduce the amount of individual effort required to reply to an email during a deep focus session. Your personal autoresponder has to be tactical with coworkers and cannot be used on your boss the majority of the time. Simply state the specific project you are working on that day and the exact details. Tell them that if it's urgent they can walk over to your office or desk where they will be greeted with a deep focus sign on the door or see earplugs in your if you're working from an open office plan. At the end of the autoresponder, tell them when you will be logging on again. Once you respond to emails at perhaps 1pm set up a new auto responder to tell them your next specific project that you'll be working on and when you will be checking emails again that evening. This is right before you leave the office just to put out any fires before you go home and be with the family. After checking your emails in the evening, set your new autoresponder for the night/morning. Usually a specific description of what you are doing and to make them actually Find you is a large enough deterrent until the next email dedicated time block. Always include the reason you have set up an autoresponder in the autoresponder. The main reason you will tell your coworkers and boss is to improve the efficiency of the company. Making your reason for not responding seem like a personal benefit will not help your case. In the autoresponder always make sure to update your new autoresponder after an email time block in the evening before going home otherwise you will look unorganized in the eyes of your coworkers. The only person that is able to get through to you is your boss during deep focus time blocks. After you talk to them about your company goal-oriented work schedule they will be more hesitant to distract you hopefully. Every couple days make sure to change the format of your autoresponder to instill your image of being proactive with your team.

You will have to renegotiate your professional relationships to better implement your new goal-oriented work method. If a coworker needs to interrupt a focus block for any reason in the future, simply tell them that you can't make plans because you have a meeting. Avoid telling them that you want to focus or are occupied with a task because then that will give them wiggle room to argue with you potentially. People take you seriously when they think you have a meeting during that time.

Environmental Noise

While background noise can have a very subjective effect on an individual's concentration, there are certain kinds of noises that are proven to diminish productivity. The most common and detrimental noise is intermittent speech. Intermittent speech is the stopping and starting of voices around you especially if it's only a hand full of people. The larger the group of people talking, the better because all the voices blend together into a larger noise. The problems arise when you can hear each conversation wholly or even just bits and pieces. These sounds distract you completely from your chain of thought because they are constantly changing and intriguing to listen to. Intermittent speech is usually impossible to prevent in areas that coworkers are present and can be found quite commonly around offices. They obviously can be eliminated from your workspace in a quiet corner of the office building. However, the most common way to combat this major distraction is to tune out the noise in a work appropriate fashion.

Whether you work in a cubicle setting or an open floor layout there are still a few techniques you want to use to minimize intermittent speech noises. You have two options that I encourage you to experiment with individually to find what works best for you. If you are the type that focuses best in complete silence then a high-quality pair of custom-fit earplugs could do the job for you. Lower quality ones will not filter out all the noise, rendering them useless. Your second and my personal favorite option is to use noise canceling headphones specifically paired with a brown noise track or isochronic tones. The Mozart effect suggests that listening to classical music can increase one's spatial-temporal reasoning along with figuring out solutions to longer problems. However, scientists have found that the Mozart effect is pure pseudoscience and refuted as basically bupkis despite entire 15 yearlong industries being born over this study who sold Mozart CD's to pregnant mothers. However, that doesn't mean we should throw away the chance of certain types of music enhancing our concentration along with the science to back up these new studies.

Basically, there are studies done that show the effects of music enhancing productivity and studies showing that it hinders productivity. Concluding that it depends on your attention span and personality whether it will help you or not. Researchers from a lab in Glasgow, Scotland, have theorized that introverts who are more easily overwhelmed by stimuli are better off working in silence than an extrovert. But we can't conclude this answer too simply despite all the research. Basically, music that stays consistent, has no intermittent speech, and is familiar is the only music that enhances deep focus. Restrictions on music are not as important when using music for exercise or creative endeavors compared to fresh and complex knowledge tasks. Upbeat music can boost physical output, while familiar, calm and consistent music is good for cognitive concentration. Therefore, music can aid in training for sports but is not very effective for reading. We want the noise to fade into the background and not be the center of attention.

Researchers from universities in Sweden, Norway and the UK in 2010 found a strong connection between, white noise, and the effects of concentration on students who have ADHD. Inattentive students are more efficient at cognitive tasks when exposed to moderate level white noises while "normal" functioning students perform worse. For me personally on my journey of conquering attentive deficit I have found that brown noise helps me focus the best compared to the other colors of noise. It is almost impossible to find a place with no noise and custom fit ear plugs do not filter out all noises. White noise is the collection of most noise frequencies in equal proportions. White noise can best be described as static coming from a television and can come across as harsh sounding. Brown noise is much softer and is of the lowest frequencies. It sounds like a soft deep waterfall, stream or light thunder. Pink noise is deeper than brown noise and described as flat or even. Pink noise can be compared to rustling leaves, steady rain, or wind and is studied to be most effective for sleep. The biggest benefit to using headphones or earplugs is that your coworkers are given a visual cue that you are busy which is especially helpful in an open floor office plan.

Isochronic tones are scientifically proven frequencies that can alter the dominant frequency of your brain to maximize your productive output and aid in minimizing distractions. Isochronic tones can be overlaid with brown noise and I highly suggest experimenting with this combination on your favorite music or video streaming service. More on isochronic tones in chapter 11.

Seeking Solitude

For any workspace related solutions to work, you need to develop the habit of actively seeking solitude. You must find a secret working spot that suits you and dedicate it entirely to work. Successful people use all kinds of obscure workspaces to focus deeply. JK Rowling famously wrote in a 5-star penthouse suite while writing her final book from her last series. Many writers and business executives go on round trip flights around the world just to have a quiet place to focus. However, airplanes are not easily accessible for all income groups. Many business executives with the money know the value of a quiet place to work free of distraction so they will happily fork over thousands. Some cheap yet effective alternatives are coffee shops, private rooms, public or university libraries, and internet cafes. I personally adore being creative and finding a unique and effective workspace. Your ideal workspace is defined by your imagination.

Summary

Minimizing your life down to the essential both mentally and physically is a rewarding process that most start in resistance and eventually fall in love with. Understanding the principle of 'less is more' is more than simply decluttering your desk. Singularity is not just a lifestyle, in moderation it is an art. Having a completely decluttered brain, body, environment and life system centered on the essential feels exuberating from the inside out.

Action Steps

- Clear your work area of all physical clutter.
- Clear your phone, and computer of digital clutter.
- Inform your co-workers of your new commitment to your goal and explain to them that it may take you longer to get back to them on emails. Tell them that they can contact you during certain select hours for optimal efficiency and progress of the company. If you are allowed, use an email autoresponder.
- Buy daylight full spectrum bulbs or a lamp to put in an area where you need deep focus.
- Invest in custom-fit earplugs, noise-canceling headphones, or if you are allowed neither, use a brown noise machine in your office.
- If you have the luxury, close your office door and put a 'Focusing Deep' sign outside to minimize disruptions.

5

PRIME YOUR BIOLOGY FOR FOCUS

Our biological makeup isn't outside of our control – there are many things that we can do to make sure we are focused for long periods. The most important component in ensuring that your brain cooperates with your need for concentration is by optimizing your biology for mastering concentration. Upgrading our biology is like upgrading the hardware of our brain supercomputer. Up until this point in the book, we have been upgrading the software of our mental supercomputer. Our brains are shaped and molded by the daily activities we do and the fuel it consumes. it determines what kind of behavior we are likely to display and how we act 'naturally.' Some people are just great at concentrating naturally, and that's because their brains on a biological level allow them to work for a longer period of time.

The brain's ability to concentrate is directly contingent on the amount of energy it can channel into the task at hand. Even when the brain is at rest, performing normal activities like breathing, and drinking takes 20% of the body's energy in the form of glucose; this makes the brain the most energy-consuming organ of the body. All of this energy goes into ensuring that the brain system is up and running, meaning that neurons can communicate with each other effectively and efficiently. When we push our brain to perform more cognitively complex tasks, the brain requires even more energy. So, if you want to concentrate more, you have to prime your body to ensure that the brain's energy requirements are being fulfilled. For example, championship chess players lose a lot of weight during a single game because they have to concentrate for up to 8 hours while their brain is burning 20% of their calories.

Sleep Routine

This is often undervalued especially in today's society of hustlers and dream builders. Sleeping as little as possible is almost a badge of honor for many knowledge workers and entrepreneurs. Sleep is extremely important because it is like running your computer to the max and not clearing your RAM or working memory. Reset your brain by getting 8 hours of sleep to clear your mind of clutter. Researchers at Boston University in Massachusetts found cerebrospinal fluid that washes in and out of the brain helping rid of metabolic waste during deep sleep cycles. If you want to build a brain that will focus effortlessly then make sleep a higher priority. Sleep helps us to keep our head clear, remember information, make smarter decisions and learn quicker. When we don't get enough sleep, our "executive functions" start to become impaired, harming our productivity. Executive functions are the functions that are monitored by the prefrontal cortex. The functions include, monitoring one's self, problem solving, working memory, learning, inhibition, starting a task, planning, decision making, concentration and resisting temptations. Basically all the skills I didn't have as an

ADD child.

According to the National Sleep Foundation, during sleep, our brain prepares for the next day by pushing memory and information from short-term to long-term storage, the connections between brain cells are strengthened, and memories are reactivated. All of this combined helps us to think faster and better and ensures that our memory banks aren't burdened, which helps us to recall and store information.

Many individuals struggle with falling asleep quickly. The best way to induce sleep even when you don't feel like it is by building a routine to trigger sleep. A routine is the best way for you to prime your body so that certain activities cue the brain to enter sleep mode. Once you start following the routine, all you have to do is carry out the steps, and your body will start to feel sleepy. Steps you must follow in a sleeping routine are:

1. Light prevents us from feeling sleepy since it keeps our brains awake by demanding our attention. Before you sleep, avoid bright or blue lights like full-spectrum bulbs, phones, or computers.

2. Get a pair of blue light filtering glasses or download an app on all of your devices to filter out blue light 1 hour before bed at least.

3. If you read physical books at night, get an amber reading light. I personally prefer a backlit electronic e-reader that doesn't emit blue light. Blue light is light emitted from electronics and is proven to wake us up and slow the production of natural melatonin in our minds. Reading is a

trained cue for my brain to fall asleep.

Taking sleep seriously means tracking our sleep and analyzing our data. Invest in a wearable sleep tracking watch or ring for best results. These devices track the length of sleep cycles your body enters and how efficiently you slept. These devices will present all your sleeping data to you organized and with tips on how to improve their depth and quality. Diving into my own personal sleeping data is so rewarding because I find days that I sleep significantly less but I become more well rested. Now I am more equipped to emulate the same results, reaching the state of sleeping less but deeper for maximum time hacking.

Water

Water is not just the source of life, but also the source of focus and clearing mental fog. Most people, who don't pay attention to what they're putting in their body, tend to ignore the importance of water and instead drink sugary or caffeinated drinks that can cause dehydration. Dehydration, even if in small amounts, can lead to a loss of concentration, and the more people consume sugary drinks, the more exhausted they become. Try keeping a bottle of water with you to keep yourself hydrated to ensure maximum concentration before going for coffee.

Water allows your brain to think faster and work more efficiently because your brain is 75% water. Your brain also needs water to absorb nutrients and remove toxins so that you can think more clearly and process huge amounts of information. You are allowed to have other beverages than water, but whenever you have a cup of tea or coffee, just make sure that you compensate for the dehydration that you are going to experience by drinking at least 2 glasses of water.

Learn to spot if you're dehydrated or not by studying your cognitive energy level. If your head feels foggy, and unable to concentrate; you are probably dehydrated.

Exercise

Moderate exercise is essential to changing the biological makeup of your brain, allowing it to concentrate for longer periods. A University of British Columbia study suggests that regular exercise increases the hippocampus area of the brain, improving your long-term memory storage. The brain is a fickle organism, and, as we age, our thinking skills, as well as the memory, slowly start eroding if we don't manage our mental biology. Exercise ensures that the brain can protect itself from memory loss and cognitive decline. The study suggested that there are specific kinds of exercises, such as regular aerobic exercises to get your heart and sweat glands pumping, which in turn have an impact on the size of the hippocampus.

There are both direct and indirect reasons for why exercise has such an impact on our memory capacity. When it comes to direct impacts – exercise reduces insulin resistance, inflammation, and stimulates the growth of nutrients that allow brain cells to become healthier and function better. Indirectly, exercises generally keep you healthy by reducing depression and anxiety, while improving mood and sleep, all of which help us to think clearly.

These are the long-term mental benefits that you can get out of exercising. We will discuss the short-term benefits in detail later on in chapters 8 and 9.

Concentration Diet

Your diet has a huge impact on the functioning of your brain. The nutritional composition of your diet directly determines how well your brain can focus. Some nutrients like carbohydrates are good for producing energy if consumed in small portions, but eating a large number of carbs in one sitting can make you feel lethargic and slow down your brain temporarily. This is why it's essential to consume the right nutrients and in the right quantity during work days. Consuming high levels of protein is also good for you – protein is essential for muscle and cell formation. It also helps to improve memory retention, recall, and alertness.

The best way to give your brain an energy boost is through MCT oil. It is an easily available supplement that people add to their smoothies, coffees, or as a salad dressing. If you use some of it every day, it'll keep you focused and ready for whatever work you may have. The full name of MCT oil is medium-chain triglyceride oil. Unlike other sources of energy, MCT oil doesn't need to be broken down to be used as fuel; instead, it can go directly to your liver bypassing the gut and give an instant energy boost. MCT oil is derived mostly from coconuts. Add MCT oil to your matcha green tea or favorite coffee to get the benefits of both.

The Glycemic Index (GI) is a comparative ranking of different carbohydrates based on their ability to affect blood glucose levels. Carbs that have a low GI value are digested, absorbed, and metabolized slowly and therefore, lead to a rise in blood glucose levels. If you do want to consume carbs, then make sure that you only consume items with a low Glycemic Index value for better executive brain functioning. According to a study conducted by Cambridge University on the eating and energy patterns of 14-year-olds, the kids who consumed low glycemic index foods had better executive function throughout the day on a the Stroop and the Flanker cognitive tests. These kids had better cognitive functioning than those who consumed high glycemic index foods or did not have breakfast at all. The primary benefits that you will get from such foods occur about 2 hours after you consume a meal. So, remember to eat meals that are in the '40s of the glycemic index. However, you have to take some precautionary measures because not all foods that have a low glycemic index are good for your health. During a deep focus session, make sure to have nutrient dense, quick and easy snacks on hand to keep your brain fueled. Meal prepping for the whole week, is also incredibly helpful for keeping us more focused on work and less on finding food. Simple clean energy and reduced decision making from meal prepping is the goal.

Natural Nootropics

Nootropics are drugs, supplements, and other similar substances that help increase cognitive function, improve memory retention, streamline executive functions like creativity, and motivation. Synthetic nootropics can be dangerous for your body, which is why it's better to go for tried and true naturally occurring supplements. My favorite and the most highly effective natural nootropics are:

Lion's Mane Mushroom

This nootropic has roots in ancient Chinese medicine and is a natural antioxidant. It supports brain health through the growth stimulation of two critical compounds: NGF (nerve growth factor) and BDNF (brain-derived neurotrophic factor). Both of these are proteins that push the brain to grow new cells and strengthen the already existing synapses. It also fights against brain degradation, memory loss, and improves mood and focus.

Acetyl L Carnitine

ALCAR is a naturally occurring amino acid within your body and is burned to generate energy. It can also act as a protein supplement to help boost your executive functions. It has two main benefits: first, it's an anti-aging nootropic that keeps your brain in shape, helping it perform better. Second, it can easily pass through the blood-brain barrier, and once it reaches your brain, it improves memory, learning, and focus.

Bacopa Monnieri

This plant is also known as Brahmi or water hyssop and is a staple plant used in Ayurvedic medicine, which is one of the world's oldest holistic medical systems that the primary Indian medical system still uses. Bacopa monnieri grows underwater, and its primary benefit is that it increases brain function. A study conducted on mice concluded that using this plant increased their ability to retain information and improve their spatial learning.

Grape Seed

Grape Seed has been famous since ancient Greece and is a universal symbol for vitality. Grape seed extract enhances brain cell growth in the hippocampus region and protects against neurodegenerative diseases. Overall increasing memory retention and focus.

Choline

Choline is a nutrient essential for brain functioning – it helps produce a neurotransmitter known as acetylcholine, which is important for learning and mental focus. Many foods are rich in choline, such as egg yolks, beef, salmon, cauliflower, etc.

Huperzine A

It is found in Chinese club moss and traditionally is used to clear the mind. Small and regular doses of Huperzine A improved memory retention and learning performance. It also increases acetylcholine signaling, which improves mental endurance.

Rhodiola Rosea

Rhodiola is an herb that grows on steep mountains and is used by people to reduce stress. A study conducted on 56 physicians working night duty concluded that Rhodiola reduced mental fatigue and helped improve work performance.

Matcha Green Tea

Matcha green tea boosts your executive functions and stops cognitive decline. It contains caffeine, which gives a boost in energy but does come with its side effects of anxiety and sleeplessness for some. Theanine is also included in matcha green tea and promotes relaxation without sedation. It helps your cognitive abilities, without making you feel over-stimulated. It is a great replacement for coffee because the caffeine and theanine combine to produce a synergistic, relaxed, zen focus, perfect for conquering your goals.

Ginkgo Biloba

Also known as maidenhair, it is a tree that is native to China. Its benefits are geared towards stopping cognitive decline and improving mental performance.

Before you decide to add any of these foods to your diet, remember to consult your doctor to see if it would be a good fit for your body. Research how these medicines will affect you personally. There are also many focus geared supplements available on the market that are a mix of different ingredients, but the disadvantage is that you don't get to experiment with each ingredient individually to learn how it affects you on a personal level.

You can't know for sure which ones will help you focus, and which won't, so separate them and test them yourself to get a clearer idea of which ones work best with your body. Some nootropics, such as grapeseed and bacopa monnieri, are not approved by the FDA. However, they have been in use for centuries by ancient civilizations from Greece to China.

Plant Based Oil Concentrates

According to Amy Galper, a board-certified aromatherapist, our sense of smell has a huge impact on different parts of our brain. When we smell something, the aromatic molecules send electrical signals to the limbic system, which helps us to learn and remember. So, when you smell a plant-based concentrate oil, it triggers your limbic system that helps to change your mood, behavior, and cognitive functioning.

Every essential oil has its very own chemical

composition that impacts your brain differently when its aroma interacts with your neurons. If you want to use oils to focus, find oils that have a balancing and calming odor. If you want a boost of energy, you can use oils like grapefruit or spearmint.

Focus enhancing oils:

- Rosemary: The aroma of rosemary helps in detoxifying and gives our brain profound clarity.
- Peppermint: If you need a stimulating boost because you feel tired, the best essential oil to try is Peppermint.
- Grapefruit: Grapefruit essential oil can be used to recharge your brain and give yourself a boost of energy.

Use an oil diffuser in your office or rub on areas of the body that have many nerve endings such as the ears or feet. Always buy high quality oils because the lower quality ones have fillers and additives.

Body Posture

Your posture determines how you look at yourself and how your brain perceives you. By using body posture, you can trick your brain into releasing chemicals that help you focus better. According to a study done by a Dutch behavioral scientist, Erik Peper, when we sit upright, we are more likely to recall positive memories and think positively in general. Our energy levels can also be maintained by keeping up a good posture; a slumped posture decreases our degree of energy. It also leads to an increase in good hormones that help us to fight disease and decrease cortisol, the stress hormone.

Summary

Priming your biology for focus will make a world of difference in altering your mind. Prioritize sleeping well despite what your colleagues say. Avoid blue light and excessive water before bed. Form a nightly ritual that triggers your brain for focus. Upon waking up make sure you drink plenty of water to avoid mental fatigue. When experiencing a dip in energy, experiment with moderate cardio and a low glycemic meal. Consider trying a couple nootropics instead of traditional focus medication and watch your life change. Finally use body posturing to feel empowered, confident and attentive.

Action Steps

- Build a high-quality nighttime routine.
- Sleep deep and sufficiently. Start tracking hours of sleep every night in a journal or excel sheet. If you own a sleep tracking watch or ring the included app will automate that for you.
- Eat focus foods, keep stable blood sugar, consume high protein and lower carb meals more frequently.
- Meal prep your meals for 4-7 days at a time. This reduces decision fatigue, time spent obtaining and making food.
- Buy quick healthy snacks and have quality protein powder on hand for deep focus sessions.
- Have a big water bottle at your desk at all times and avoid going to the water cooler.
- Consult with your medical professional about taking natural nootropics.
- Experiment with oil blends geared towards focus.
- Use body posturing to feel confident and focused.

PHASE 2: FOCUSING DEEP - STARTING YOUR DAY OF ULTIMATE FOCUS

6

HOW TO PLAN YOUR PERFECT ROUTINE FOR ULTIMATE FOCUS

"Give me 6 hours to chop down a tree, and I will spend the first hour sharpening the ax."

ABRAHAM LINCOLN

Planning Your Schedule

Planning your schedule is the most important practical aspect of integrating an intentional attention lifestyle. It can also become complicated because a single schedule cannot fit everyone's needs and, therefore, can't be promoted as the best schedule to follow for productivity. You must use the guidelines listed in this chapter to discover your own personal routine. Winston Churchill used to work late into the night and then break up his daytime with naps, while Toni Morrison would wake up early in the morning to write. Your schedule needs to accommodate your strengths and weaknesses, but also your interests and your overall mental and physical capacities. You must identify those aspects of your life, which bring you the most value and joy and systematically eliminate the aspects that don't. Prioritize working less but with deeper focus, removing as much maintenance work as possible while keeping a positive image at work. Then remove recreational activities that don't make you happy or align with your higher purpose. Creating the perfect prioritized work life balance.

Deep Focus Blocks

Focus blocking is also called the time blocking method and is incredibly popular in the time management space. We are calling it focus blocking because the center of attention is our hours spent in deep focus on goal work every day. A focus block is simply a planned period where you deliver your highest level of concentration. We want to work smart not hard. Brute force techniques for solving work problems may increase our threshold for attention in the long term however, if overdone it will lead to burnout. Working intelligently is always the priority as opposed to brute force. Focus blocks are the pillars holding up our careers and protecting our valued time off. Protect them relentlessly. For a focus block, it is important to leave the distraction of your phone somewhere out of reach, such as in your car when you arrive to work or in another room if you work from home. You can always go back for it if required. When you are a knowledge worker who always works on a schedule, keeping a phone on you is the equivalent of Usain Bolt, gold medalist sprinter, eating 5 pizzas right before an Olympic race. You are bound to slow down and lose the race. Your focus blocks need to be defended and protected as if your entire career depends on it because, in many ways, it does.

As for the length of the focus block, it is important to start small and gradually build the duration. A good time to start with is a 55-minute focus block followed by a 5-minute break. Many individuals struggle with sustaining deep high-quality focus for 55 minutes. If that is the case then try 25- minute focus blocks with 5-minute break.

According to Gloria Mark, who studies digital distractions at the University of California, attention residue to the last task we did typically lasts for 23 minutes and 15 seconds. Even a 10-second email fueled distraction can turn into 23 minutes of being out of focus due to attention residue. This is why a focus block needs to be completely immune to all possible distractions. To make any actual progress, you will need longer focus blocks because it takes more neurons to start a new task. You can move from the initial 55 minutes to 110 minutes with 5-minute breaks, and so on. I aim for all my deep focus sessions to be between 2-4 hours with mini minute breaks and a 15-minute break after. You must take a slightly longer break in between focus sessions. Utilize these times for meals. Breaks also need to be utilized well to maximize the use of focus blocks by only doing specific resting tasks. To look at ways breaks must be used well, refer to Chapter 9: Mental Energy Management.

Plan Every Minute From Nothing to Massive Action

Planning everything down to the minute is an intimidating yet effective routine building strategy. This includes fun, hobbies, creative work, and work breaks. You need to also delegate a block of time every day to doing nothing. This might sound like an odd suggestion in a book about productivity, but down time gives the brain time to think about plans, recharge and solve problems. Whenever you are in the middle of a focus block, you don't have time to contemplate about your plans for the day. During this period, your mind will immediately start to work on solutions for problems that might have cropped up during the day. You must schedule your longer daydream blocks near the end of the day. In a tired state, your mind is more open to creative ideas which will aid your problem-solving abilities.

With the help of this daydream block, you will get a better perspective on your intentions, and priorities in life. A study published in the Proceedings of the National Academy of Sciences tried to locate how the brain works when it is supposedly 'dormant.' It found that the problem-solving parts of the brain are extremely active during these periods of down time. Daydreaming is a state where the brain has potential to switch from the tasks at hand to the bigger problems in your life. We are more prone to slip into this state when we are mentally exhausted or stuck. Daydreaming is most useful when making a life altering decision, solving a problem, or doing creative work. Keep a physical notepad to record all the ideas and plans that come to you during the daydream block. Keeping a separate notebook is important so that you can study your ideas without any distractions and apply them back to your work. Extreme 'busy-ness' can also be equated to laziness. This is because extreme busy behavior is a chaotic state, which is usually the result of poor prioritization, poor decision-making, and a lack of attention to the present. This is one of the downfalls of the 'hustle mode' mentality. It's viewed as a badge of honor in our society. Planning to do nothing is not lazy as long as literally nothing is done except sitting, walking and thinking about life or work.

Anticipating Emotions

Try to anticipate the emotions that certain tasks will evoke and plan your schedule accordingly. For example, if you know that a meeting or a public appearance is likely to induce anxiety, then exercising right before will boost your energy and confidence. Try socializing with friends before a difficult meeting to keep you happy. Similarly, if you have a lot of free time on a flight or a car ride, you can use that as a daydream block.

Morning Ritual

It is necessary to tackle the most important task of the day first thing in the morning when you are fresh. Some people who are not used to waking up early can use many techniques to help their transition. Always leave your phone charging in a different room overnight so that it does not become a distraction in the morning. To wake up, use a physical alarm or an AI assistant speaker. You could also consider jumping in a cold shower or pool. Honestly cold water for me wakes me up far more and quicker than stimulants ever will. This is a tested technique for an instantly fresh morning. You could experiment with keeping your favorite caffeine product by your bedside to help get you up on those early morning grind sessions. You must also have full-spectrum lights in your bedroom, which you turn on the moment you wake up.

Consistency is key when it comes to maintaining your daily and weekly plans. Constantly reviewing your schedule helps you track your progress and build automatic habits. Always plan your day the night before to reduce decision fatigue in the morning. Mornings are for massive action, not delegation. A few tasks must always be done in the evening in order to protect your sacred focus blocks. Have your lunch for work prepared, daily chores done, and work clothes chosen. Many successful individuals swear by exercising first thing in the morning and I suggest that for people who prioritize fitness as their main life goal or people that struggle to make it happen after work. However, since everything is easier in the morning, I need to work smart not hard and do my most complex or creative work first thing in the morning. I experience diminishing returns on my time investment when trying to do my high priority deep focus work in the evening to make up for lost time. Save the more mindless tasks for the evening.

The most important task that needs to be completed in the evening is planning your next work day. Now is the time to check your emails and figure out what your most important priority is for the next day. Prioritize all your tasks as 1, 2, and 3 with the tasks ranked as one being the highest in terms of how early you need to finish them. Try to single your priorities for the day down to 5-3. To a busy executive this may seem impossible however using singularity will boost the quality of your output. Anything else done during the day after that is a bonus.

Theodore Roosevelt's daily routine has often been called ruthlessly efficient and is a great example of someone who consistently works hard and plays hard. Being a politician, a passionate outdoorsman, and a connoisseur of great speeches, could not have been managed at the same time if it were not for his strict routine. During his years as a student he was able to get a tremendous amount of work done in very little time by simply focusing deeper than his peers, he was able to accomplish more in less time. This intricate routine was religiously followed and used to handle a very fine balance of work and creative pursuits and clearly worked for Theodore Roosevelt. What is striking about it is that most activities were scheduled for a half-hour to one-hour period. The majority of his time was spent giving speeches; however, his time chunks were small and wedged between time blocks of maintenance work. By approaching his day like this, he was able to get a lot of goal work as well as maintenance work done. There is not much in the world that cannot be achieved with a good routine and the tenacity to see it through. Visualize your master daily plan as a series of small tasks done well, they will become much more manageable and approachable.

Summary

When making your perfect routine for focus, make sure to track your time to understand where it is going. Prioritize your focus blocks before anything else. Plan every minute of your week and don't let your goals fall to chance. When planning, anticipate emotions elicited from certain tasks and plan healthy coping mechanisms in your calendar. Set yourself up for the next day, the night before to reduce decision fatigue. Form a sacred morning ritual to take charge of the most important time of the day.

Action Steps

- Write down what the three most important work and leisure priorities in your life are. They must be put somewhere visible such as your phone lockscreen or workspace wall.

- Track your time for a week. To track it, you could use an app on your phone, or go the traditional way and write in a journal.

- Download a calendar app that syncs between your phone and computer.

- Download a to-do list app. On this app, create separate lists for the day, week and month. Every night create a to-do list for the following day and prioritize 5-3 of the most important tasks as 1, 2, or 3.

- Have your daily time chunking plan from your calendar viewable at all times. Either print it out or have it visible on your personal computer.

- Use notifications from your computer calendar to alert you when you move on to the next block. Set all your reminders to go off at the same time that the calendar event ends. This is because you don't want to be checking the time as it interrupts the flow of your work. If you need time to prepare for the next focus block, plan a preparatory time beforehand.

- At the end of your work day plan your next day by doing all chores, set up your clothes, and lunch. Then make a list of your 3-5 priorities for the next day.

- Start a productivity journal. Write down everything you complete that brings you closer to your goal. Have separate sections each project and sub sections for tracking goal work and maintenance work. Schedule weekly reviews and check to make sure that you are fulfilling your top three life priorities.
- On Sunday night, plan your following week. For each task, set up a reward that you will receive at the completion, as mentioned in chapter 2. The goal is to do less work with more focus.

7

DISTRACTION IS NOT EVIL

"The strongest principle of growth lies in human choice"

GEORGE ELIOT

What is a Necessary Distraction?

Ancient humans weren't built to work for long hours without getting distracted. We eventually evolved from needing distractions to craving them. There are times when we simply cannot avoid being distracted, but this doesn't mean that we can't utilize this distraction to help us in our path towards intentionality. Sometimes your spouse may call you, the kids may need food, or you'll have to simply go to the bathroom. You must utilize this necessary moment of distraction to do or delegate tasks that might distract you later, like grabbing a glass of water or reexamining the task at hand.

Use this moment of distraction to your advantage by alienating yourself from what you were working on and thinking about it. Take a moment to think about whether what you're currently working on is what will help you fulfill your goals. Is this the best use of your mental energy? See it as a creativity break where you go over your work and review it to see if you want to make any changes; this is also the time when a great idea might strike that will help you complete the work faster. Take the time out to make adjustments to the plan of your day. Decision-making takes a lot of energy, even if we don't realize it. By using the otherwise wasted energy on using necessary distractions to contemplate, you will save time and energy.

Why Are Necessary Distractions Helpful?

Making choices one at a time is simple but could be compounded into a difficult process that potentially causes mental fatigue as discussed earlier. Past president Obama is also famous for only wearing blue and grey suits to reduce decisions. Choices determine who we become in the future, and therefore it can be exhausting to ponder over them. That is why the majority of what we do becomes a routine that we conduct on autopilot. All of your decision moments must be planned out in advance so that you don't waste time and energy on them. But this doesn't mean that circumstances will always agree with you; life is likely to throw curveballs at you. If you use these moments of distraction to your advantage, then they can be used in your favor. Stick to the plan that you have, but use these moments to think wisely. Ideally, between your newly cultivated habits and your daily and weekly plans, you won't have to waste energy on making decisions. This will ensure that your focus does not stray from the goals you wish to achieve.

Feel Out the Decision Moment

When these necessary distractions hit, we need to feel out the moment using metacognition. Metacognition is being aware of one's own thought processes granting you control over your psyche. You become more mindful of your thoughts, eliminating negative thought processes and clutter from your brain.

Most people don't think about what they're doing and thinking; they just go along with whatever is happening. Becoming aware of yourself is essential to change who you are and how you function. You can't build focus without asking yourself important questions about your status as a being – ask yourself what you are feeling and why. Are you using your energy strategically with the current task you are doing? What is the most important task you have to do right now? Human beings aren't machines; we must be tactical about how we expend our mental resources instead of always using brute force. The most productive activity you can do is to clear out your head and emotions before you move on to the next task. You can do this by walking, breathing deep, and moderate exercise.

If you get interrupted and can't come back to work immediately, don't lose your thinking process. Write everything down before you leave the workstation so you can pick up where you left off later. You might need this when, for example, the kids ask you to do something for them, and you have to leave your work.

Utilize the Decision Moment

We have multiple moments during a day when we get distracted, ideally, we already have planned these out in between our focus blocks. However sometimes when a distraction comes our way anyway it's best to use it to our advantage by taking a 5-minute recharge break. Time that we can just sit and breathe. Experiment with taking energy inducing breaks for water, caffeine, or a quick run up the stairs. This will be helpful because these distractions can be utilized as a break to help us to clear our minds and give us energy. This ensures that the most important task is done to our highest ability.

If your mind is wandering, then you're not connected at that moment to what you're doing, and forcing yourself to work only makes you lose more energy. So, let your mind wander and use that moment to think creatively about the tasks or work problems you have at hand. Mind-wandering is extremely helpful because it allows us to think creatively about our problems. You can allow your mind to wander by looking out of the window or at pictures in your office space. There are multiple situations that we encounter that require us to think outside the box. Psychologists at the University of California, Santa Barbara, have discovered that such out of the box, creative thinking has a process behind it. The only time we can think creatively is when we take a break from the work we're supposed to do. We need to be intentional about our focus block breaks otherwise creativity may not strike. Try simply sitting, or walking instead of the main task, your mind will start to think creatively about how to solve the original problem. Sometimes doing easier but important work at hand is the best form of a break.

This doesn't mean that all kinds of mind wandering, and distractions are good. If you encounter a thought that isn't about the task at hand, let that thought pass by.

Plan the Next Choice Moment in the Future

Whenever distraction strikes, use that moment to think about any choice you might have to make in the future. Planning for the future helps us in conserving mental energy when we need it most because we have already encountered the problem before and thought of the solution. When your brain encounters a new problem, it takes valuable energy to process and find a solution. By making choices well in advance, you won't have to waste your energy when trying to focus deeply.

Summary

When a necessary distraction arises feel out the moment. View your project from the big picture, is this task the most progressive expenditure of my time? Utilize the moment of distraction, making the best decision for your mental energy and focus.

Action Steps

- When a choice moment arises, try to find a way to plan for that in the future, if possible.
- Practice relieving emotions when they arise for maximum efficiency.
- Be mindful of your choices.
- Keep a notepad and pen nearby to jot down where you left off in case you have a necessary distraction.

8

ENTERING THE DEEP STATE – THE MYSTICAL STATE OF ACHIEVEMENT

Professor of psychology and management Mihaly Csikszentmihalyi is recognized globally for coining the term 'flow' for the state of extreme productivity, happiness and mindfulness. He describes it as "being completely involved in an activity for its own sake. The ego falls away. Time flies. Every action, movement, and thought follows inevitably from the previous one, like playing jazz. Your whole being is involved, and you're using your skills to the utmost." The flow phenomenon is often experienced by extreme sport athletes, painters, writers and knowledge workers from all walks of life. In this chapter I am going to refer to the flow state as the deep state because deep focus is our priority. The same principles for extreme sport athletes are true for, executives, entrepreneurs and students. Flow is described by Professor Csikszentmihalyi as a state that we can enter while doing any activity in life that fits a certain criterion. The deep state for this chapter is specifically a state that we enter when our highest quality work flows out of us efficiently with minimal effort. This can be achieved if you are doing an activity that you are good at and that brings you great happiness.

There are a few things that are necessary to attaining a deep state.

- Having a clear, concrete idea about what you are going to do in the deep state.
- Have an adequately challenging goal.
- Eliminating all distractions from your environment and your mind.
- Aim to feel joyful.
- Surround yourself with a familiar or novel environment.

There is an intricate link between the deep state and happiness, it appears that human beings are at their happiest when they are entirely immersed into a difficult but rewarding task.

The Neuroscience of Diving Deep

There are many neuroanatomical changes in the brain that make the deep state possible. Surprisingly, when the brain is supposedly working at its best, it is slowing down and experiencing transient hypofrontality – a phenomenon where the working memory parts of the brain such as the prefrontal cortex are less active. During deep states, the brain produces a vast quantity of norepinephrine, serotonin, endorphins, anandamide, and dopamine. All these chemicals are connected to performance enhancement. The brain is always in a state of waking consciousness, but in the deep state, the brainwaves are somewhere between this default waking state and the empty, daydreaming state. This is the state of being fully connected to the present moment.

The deep state is most easily induced during your biological peak time or BPT. It requires a state of high energy and low distraction and therefore is best suited for the mornings along with the times right after taking a break. Listening to your favorite happy music is very useful when triggering the deep state. Just make sure that you turn it off once you start working. You must listen to the right kind of music as you work on a very specific task. The perfect amount of caffeine is a very useful tool for aiding in triggering deep focus. These are necessary tips for building a pre-deep ritual but the most value comes from personalization. Many successful athletes use ultra-specific pre deep focus rituals to get in the zone before an important performance.

Synthetic Memories for Focus

When Michael Phelps was a teenager, his coach would instruct him to go home and watch a 'videotape' before bed and on waking up. This videotape was not real and existed only in Phelps's mind. It was a mental visual of the perfect race where Phelps would imagine diving, landing beautifully, and swimming perfectly. He would replay this every morning and night in his mind. Then, during practice, the coach would instruct him to put in the videotape, which meant that Phelps had to put his perfect mental race into practice. This is an example of Phelps working on a synthetic memory. Athletes often use this mental imagery technique to attain peak physical performance by implanting a memory in their minds that they attempt to bring to life every time they practice. For Phelps, the visual and the verbal message is the trigger for his deep state.

Jack Nicklaus, World Champion Golfer, says that, "I never hit a shot, not even in practice, without having a very sharp in-focus picture of it in my head."

Brain patterns activated when visualizing a specific motor activity is similar to doing the physical exercise. Guang Yue, exercise science psychologist from the Cleveland Clinic Foundation conducted a study, displaying evidence that visualizing weight lifting is half as effective as physically weight lifting. One group of people went to lift weights and the other group of individuals carried out imaginary workouts in their minds. He found a 30% increase in the group that actually lifted and the group of individuals who conducted only mental exercises increased physical strength by 13.5%. These results stayed consistent for the 3-month long study. Similar studies suggest that simply visualizing or physically doing a task is not as effective as doing both in combination.

Imagine yourself easily diving into focus on your current challenge at work every morning and night for 5 to 10 minutes. Imagine how you overcome obstacles that come your way with minimal effort. See yourself completing it and feel the satisfaction from a job well executed. This may seem like a miniscule or unnecessary activity however the most massive progress in your concentration will be gained from this small 10-minute ritual alone.

Environmental Deep State Triggers

For a successful environmental trigger, you need to use a dedicated workspace. We need a place that is only dedicated to work similar to how our beds are only dedicated to sleep. Sleep experts recommend that people avoid hanging out or watching tv in their beds because they miss out on the psychological trigger of inducing sleep.

Another technique that triggers flow for extreme athletes is high consequence situations. For them being in the air immediately triggers adrenaline, making them more aware and alert. How does this relate to knowledge workers? A risk or a high consequence situation is not merely about putting your physical body in danger; it is also about emotional and intellectual risks. This is why some managers use fear to ignite their employees to work. The adrenaline of being let go ignites them to either work better or crumble under the pressure. However, true deep focus comes from a place of fulfillment not fear. New and novel environments induced our ancestors to be more alert. When we are struggling to trigger flow at our normal workstation, the best technique is finding a new environment to work such as a new coffee shop. Such unpredictable environments can ignite our senses, and put us into the present moment triggering the deep state. You need to strike a balance between familiarity from a routine and unpredictability in your environment to give your mind the best chance at hitting this mystical state.

Psychological Triggers

Attempt to create an atmosphere of energy and positivity to generate a mental cue, using the synthetic memory technique. Experiment with adding your favorite feel good music while reflecting on your past successes and visions for the future. Moderate cardio can also help create this mental atmosphere. It releases endorphins and dopamine in the brain, which lights up energy, focus, and reward patterns in the brain. In the immediate short term, exercise improves your focus, clears your head, makes your thoughts sharper, reduces your anxiety, and increases your self-control. Your cognitive functions become sharper, and you think of processes and solutions easier. The hippocampus, the long-term memory center of the brain, responds vehemently to light exercise. It also boosts your sense of mental wellbeing and therefore is a power tool to unleash your creative problem-solving side.

Try to disrupt the familiar patterns of the brain and approach things from a different perspective. Sometimes a new outlook on a problem can trigger a whole series of associated thoughts that will lead you to the deep focus state.

Avoid looking at the time. This prevents you from entering the deep state because you are focused on the time instead of enjoying the work at hand. For scheduling deep focus sessions, use the time blocking method described earlier. Make sure to use a physical clock or an AI-assisted timer to time your deep focus sessions. Rely on a schedule on your wall or computer to inform you of when to move on to the next event on the calendar. When you are in the flow of the deep state, don't be super rigid with your schedule if you don't have to be. Ride out the sacred flow for as long as possible.

Aftermath & Summary

When these triggers succeed in inducing a deep state in you, afterwards your task is to make the deep state stronger, deeper, and more easily attainable next time. For this, record your deep state time, what triggered it, how it made you feel, and what ideas you had while in it. This will make it easier to trigger the state in the future. With time, you will have your own deep state triggering ritual strategy to tackle any challenging aspect of your career. This will unleash a whole new realm of possibilities for efficient working. Your next promotion, bonus or level of success is now within your grasp.

Action Steps

- Create a specific deep state ritual that you do right before you enter a focus time block. For example, put your phone in a different room, listen to your favorite music, and utilize a deep-dedicated workspace. Visualize yourself completing the task and try to imagine the feeling you will get upon completing it.

- Remove watches and clocks from your line of sight and rely on calendar reminders, a timer or AI assistant speaker to remind you to move on to the next event.

- When you hit the deep state, carefully record the feelings you had, what triggered it and how you will replicate this in the future.

9

MENTAL ENERGY MANAGEMENT - THE ART OF SIMPLICITY

"Simplicity is the ultimate sophistication."

LEONARDO DA VINCI

Deep focus is not a marathon. It is a series of sprints with a brief resting period in between. In order to use our minds effectively we have to utilize our mental energy to be synergistic with our biological clock, mood, and environment.

Our minds need the proper energy to process information effectively on a day-to-day basis. The strength to perform difficult tasks is always within you, but it can get dull due to mental clutter. To reinvigorate your ability to carry out tasks, you need to declutter your mind. Mental decluttering is like rearranging a messy room – your overloaded mind needs to be reset to avoid burnout.

Mental decluttering is the act of paying attention to one task, thought or feeling in each moment. If you keep focusing on different things through the course of a task, your mind will be confused and scattered.

One of the biggest reasons for burnout is poor

organization and multitasking.

Releasing mental clutter is a transformation and necessary skill to master in order to excel in your career. Before we can understand how to release mental clutter, we must understand how our internal working memory works.

Working Memory

Working memory is a limited capacity cognitive system that can only hold several pieces of information temporarily. The term was coined by George Miller, Eugene Galanter, and Karl Pribram. It is mainly regulated by the prefrontal cortex at the frontal lobe of the brain. That is the region associated with focus, planning, decision making, and moderating one's self. The working memory of your brain is like the RAM of your computer. The efficiency of our working memory declines rapidly when it becomes full. Active decluttering and deleting of background processes in our working memory is required in order to operate at peak productivity.

Releasing Emotions to Clear Working Memory

When there is an overload of emotions, your working memory is burdened. Think of your working memory as a game of Kloski – a sliding puzzle game with a little one block space to move the puzzle pieces around. Over time your mind is overburdened by too many blocks (in our case emotions), until it fills up and there is no way to make space for solving the puzzle. The burdens of daily, personal and professional life can compound making it difficult for you to focus.

The following exercises will help you declutter the working memory and release emotions as well because emotions clog the working memory. We can't think logically when our working memory is filled with negative emotions. These techniques can be used for clearing the mind in general but are especially effective for clearing a working memory clogged with highly charged negative emotions such as anger or fear.

Exercising

Frequent moderate cardio is the easiest way to rid yourself of emotional stress. Exercise helps in the release of relaxation hormones, which help in stress management.

By performing any moderate cardio of your choice, you will be able to release daily work tensions and focus deeper afterwards.

Walking in Nature

The pace of urban life can often be disturbingly incomprehensible for our primal mind. Recent studies have tried to find a connection between exposure to nature and emotional health.

Gregory Bratman from Stanford University studied the impact of urban living on the mental health of city dwellers. His study discovered that - volunteers who walked in the green parks of Stanford were happier and less stressed as compared to volunteers crossing traffic and city lights.

Bratman also conducted a study on the effects of "brooding" on the mental health of city dwellers. Brooding or overthinking is the act of mental reflection, which is constant and overwhelming in many cases. It increases blood flow to the subgenual prefrontal cortex.

He used data from brain scans and thirty-eight questionnaires filled by city dwellers to discover levels of brooding after walking in different areas.

The volunteers who walked on highways and urban centers still had high levels of blood to the subgenual prefrontal cortex, and their brooding levels remained unchanged.

Volunteers who walked in paths filled with greenery displayed signs of improved mental health. According to their brain scans and answers in questionnaires - their attitude underwent a positive transformation. Their levels of brooding were reduced compared to those exposed to the distracting environment of the highway. The blood flow to the subgenual prefrontal cortex was less, and their brain was remarkably calmer.

Instead of going out for drinks to blow off steam, try planning a hike in nature. Invite your coworkers and hike up a mountain for the perfect de-stressor.

Ways of Releasing Mental Clutter

Mental clutter must be released to reorient your focus and rejuvenate your mental health. Breaks in concentration and short attention spans can be caused by mental cluttering. You can take up daily tasks like stretching, taking a relaxing shower, or spending time with your loved ones for mental decluttering.

Showers

Showers act as an excellent relaxant; take one after a stressful day at work, or when you want to think of new ideas. American director, writer and actor, Woody Allen, vouches for the power of a warm or cold shower in times of needed inspiration.

Allen, prefers taking a shower while he is writing a new script. It helps him rejuvenate his nerves and acts as a catalyst for new ideas in his mind. A combination of stretching and taking a short refreshing shower can help you recharge your mind and make more room for creativity.

Sharing with Loved Ones

Sometimes, sharing the cause of your anxiety and stress due to work can help you declutter your mind from negative emotions. You must seek out advice and conversation from your family, friends, or partner. Seeking out empathy can make you feel more positive and push out the negative thoughts. Be careful not to dwell on your problems for too long.

Having a Laugh

Laughing is known to have fantastic health benefits for your mood. If you feel distracted or stressed, watch a stand-up comedy show or a funny video to feel less anxious.

When you laugh, endorphins are released by your body. This boosts your immunity and lessens signs of aggression caused by a heavy workload. Many people practice laughing as an exercise for an increased life span as well.

Power Naps

The best way to rest your mind is taking a power nap. Power naps will make you more productive and focused afterwards. When you work through feeling extremely tired, the quality of your work might decrease.

Sleeping regulates decluttering of the mind. I know power naps are not acceptable usually in a professional environment. If you can find privacy in your car in the parking lot then try experimenting with a power nap. When you plan your naps, you recharge your energy quickly, without having to break the flow of a focus block later.

A nap should usually be between ten to thirty minutes to keep you alert once you wake up.

Seek Solitude

In the urbanized pace of our world, solitude has become a luxury. Solitude is an essential factor for innovation of any kind. The lack of occasional distance from others can cause overwhelm and distraction.

But in today's world of smartphones, we rarely experience true solitude, even in our alone time. We carry them around in our pockets to remain connected to the whole world with the touch of a screen, however the sense of community on social media is unsatisfying compared to in-person contact. Technology has many life-changing benefits that are productive if used mindfully, but if not used appropriately, it will add to your stress.

Solidify your views, think, focus on your inner self and broaden your perspectives by allotting time to be alone. Being alone and seeking solitude must be without any external stimuli the majority of the time.

Use your alone time to truly be one with your mind and channel your attention away from the chaos of the world temporarily.

Daydreaming

Daydreaming is an exercise that helps you to think creatively, channeling the energy of your imagination and decluttering your mind. A wandering mind can build a better "working memory," as revealed by research conducted by the University of Wisconsin and the Max Planck Institute for Human Cognitive and Brain Science. A strong working memory depicts the mind's capacity to retain and reproduce information even in the presence of distractions.

According to their research, subjects who daydreamed more had higher activity in regions of the brain associated with working memory. Therefore, we must train our minds to daydream to increase our working memory.

To daydream, your mind must be away from external noises and distractions. You must seek silence if you want to be more creative. The World Health Organization has declared "noise pollution" as an epidemic of the twenty-first century.

Problem Solving Methods

It is natural to go through a mental block while working through obstacles. Here are some techniques to push your limits and come up with solutions to problems.

Walking

When you feel stuck on a particular idea, you can take a short walk until you figure out a solution for your dilemma. Direct your thoughts to the problem at hand and keep your mind from wandering to other issues.

Set a deadline for finding the solution, but do not stop walking until you have an answer if possible.

Sitting

Try sitting in a comfortable spot with proper posture and ponder over the problem you need to understand. Breathe until you have discovered the right way to solve it. Breathing exercises will keep your mind alert and maintain continuous oxygen flow to your brain. Imagine the problem with every breath you take and direct your mind to its solution. Do not get up until you solve the problem.

Sleeping on a Problem

Many great minds in history have used sleep as an effective tool in their arsenal to tackle a mind occupying problem. Vladimir Bekhterev, Russian neuroscientist and father of objective psychology, was best known for noting the role of the hippocampus in memories. When referring to discovering solutions in his sleep, he said, "It happened several times when I concentrated in the evening on a subject which I had put into poetic shape, that in the morning, I had only taken a pen and the words flowed, as it were, spontaneously. I only had to polish them later." Otto Loewi discovered that active chemicals are involved in the action of nerves while he was sleeping. This led later to him winning the Nobel prize in 1936. These are just a couple examples of the many global knowledge workers that are using sleep to harness their creative discoveries. This is the ultimate time hack.

External Brain System

You cannot always rely on your memory alone to keep you organized and on schedule. When you store your information in an external brain system, you can revisit your action plan and make sure you do not forget anything important. Event calendars, daily to-do lists, weekly task deadlines, and monthly reviews are all tools used in your external brain system. Invest in physical or digital journals. I totally relate to people who love to keep physical notebooks and write everything out. Although, personally I only use digital notebooks because they all are organized way more efficiently and easier to refer back to. Instead of having a mountain of physical notebooks, all my notebooks fit in my computer, phone and sync seamlessly. I can search my notebooks easily using the search feature instead of flipping through pages. I would literally have 31 and counting physical notebooks if I didn't use a note taking software. You need a separate notebook for meetings, projects, must learn research topics, productivity tracking, mental health, deep state tracking, meditation, new ideas from daydreaming, personal reflection, important books to read, life goals, sleep, diet and anything else you need to remember next week or years down the road.

I also have found AI smart speakers to be extremely useful. When I first heard of them I thought they sounded gimmicky but honestly mine has changed my life. Since I keep my phone charging in a separate room to avoid decision fatigue first in the morning. I ask my speaker to tell me my daily schedule. Instead of checking the time in the middle of the night or during a deep state focus block I ask my timer to tell me the time. This way I can avoid looking at distracting screens with notifications waiting for my delegation. When I start a new deep focus block that isn't scheduled in my calendar I tell my speaker to set a timer instead of using my phone. If I am on a role in the deep state then I tell the speaker to set a stop watch to track my time so I can squeeze every ounce of efficiency from the inspiration. During a deep focus block or in the middle of the night when an amazing idea or solution to a problem strikes, I tell my speaker to remind me of this idea. I tell it what time I want to wake up every morning and it even plays ocean, cracking fire, babbling rivers or other nature sounds while I sleep. I don't advocate multitasking, although while I am doing easy chores, I tell my speaker to play audiobooks or podcasts for me. Honestly all these tasks can be done on your phone or computer obviously but the point is I am religiously cutting distraction out of my life especially during moments of sleep, deep focus and family time. I want to be fully present in the moment.

Schedule monthly reviews for your whole external brain system in order to avoid letting tasks or responsibilities slip through the cracks. The entire point of an external brain is to prevent missing a single detail, taking the load off your mind.

The point is for you to lessen the pressure of extra information and attention residue in your head and direct all the focus on work. Many people are under the illusion that this will decrease our cognitive memory however the idea is not to think of less but to focus on more by prioritizing every resource we have to the present moment task. With everything being kept track of in your external brain system through a to do list app, calendar, journals, and timers your brain is able to move mountains.

Behaviors to Avoid

Certain behaviors give us the illusion of relaxation but in reality, suck your energy completely and inhibit efficient work.

Avoid scrolling through any sort of novel stimulating media on your work breaks or first thing in the morning. The faster the scrolling the worse the side effects. Refer to chapter three for more information on how constant scrolling through media short circuits our attention to shorter time frames, training us to be distracted and depleting our mental resources. You must avoid bad habits that give the illusion of relaxation but in fact deplete our focus levels.

Whenever you feel like giving up, listen to your recorded voice speaking your affirmations and repeat them out loud to gain control of your willpower.

Another great method to avoid a tempting bad habit is to use urge surfing. This is feeling out your desire and examining why you have it. This will be discussed more in depth in the next chapter.

During work hours, long breaks will be extremely detrimental as they inhibit you from ever returning to work. The longer the break the less likely you will enter back into the deep focus mode. Your state of mind gets fixated in a relaxed state and endangers your likelihood to return back to work.

Being around friends and family gives some people energy, while draining others. It is all about finding out what recreational activities give you energy personally. What you will find is that you must prioritize your relaxation time to be as deep as possible and exactly what your mind needs to be completely rejuvenated. Movies, video games, and other mind cluttering activities are usually worse for focus than walking, laughing with friends and meditation. However, removing these activities from your life completely is not required because sometimes they can be a useful tool to gather friends and family but partaking daily alone is not recommended for concentration.

Summary

Be aware of the space in your working memory. Are you allocating resources to pent up emotions or unsolved problems? Clear your working memory with exercise, a nature walk, a shower, a laugh, power nap, seeking solitude, or day dreaming. Find solutions to your problems by sitting, walking or sleeping on them. Form an external brain productivity system to clear up your memory as well. By carefully selecting what you do during the day, you save your mental energy for focus, fulfillment and family.

Action Steps

- Review your schedule, have your deep rest breaks planned and what type of break you will be taking.
- Formulate your external brain system. You should already have a calendar, focus block timer, a to-do list, a reminder system, and in-depth software or physical notebooks.

10

EMBRACE DISCOMFORT – THE WAY OF THE WARRIOR

"The struggle alone pleases us, not the victory."

BLAISE PASCAL

The journey to ultimate focus is not one without struggle. On your path to success, you will encounter challenges that will make you feel like giving up. In times like this, it is important to remember that you must embrace the discomfort. We must shift our perspective of discomfort from being a feeling we avoid to a feeling we seek and enjoy. Accepting the misfortunes that come your way must be viewed as a way to multiply your future fortunes even further.

There is nothing more terrible than working hard every day and coming back to bed feeling disillusioned. After a hectic day of discomforting challenges in the workplace, you can feel burnt out. It is not easy to get over this feeling, and you must build mental habits of thought monitoring constantly, so your work output, focus and mental health does not suffer. It is easier to prevent burnout than to pull ourselves out of feeling burnt out especially if the corporate pressure is on.

You must remember to build focus in your life by being

attentive to your present. High pressure work environments can shut you down and take you back to your past failures. Over time you will realize programming yourself to be in the moment will help you in conquering your fears and inhibitions.

Understand that sometimes we put our happiness in front of us instead of keeping it within us. We will only allow ourselves to be happy once we finish this project, financial quarter or income goal. This is called a deferred happiness payment plan and is detrimental to your concentration.

One of the best ways to combat burnout is to bring ourselves back into the moment. The practice of being self-aware and maintaining tranquility at work despite all odds is called mindfulness. Being one hundred percent focused in the present moment allows you to still function at a high level while giving you space to relax. Simply practice sitting and breathing every morning and night to nurture this state of serenity in your mind. This exercise can be coupled with your synthetic memory exercise from the last chapter in order to synergistically amplify your tranquility and ability to focus.

Research has shown that mindfulness is a great remedy for stress reduction. It reduces the anxiety of completing tasks on time by helping you streamline the process of work. Many organizations, such as the Mayo Clinic, Google, and Adobe, have formal mindfulness programs to increase employee productivity and engagement. One of the most common causes of people quitting work is stress. Therefore, these organizations have set up healthy mindfulness practices for increased productivity, keeping the wellbeing of the employees in mind.

A survey conducted by Paychex of about two thousand

employees revealed that the most prominent cause of stress is the failure to manage work and home life at the same time. These individuals have made use of mindfulness programs to streamline their work and remain productive.

Mindfulness is based on a strategy of being fully intentional and aware. It must be applied to structuring your work day to create a healthy work balance. Mindfulness helps to build attention in every aspect of work. Therefore, it increases the absorption of information for those who are learning new skills.

Such a structured and balanced work-life facilitates creativity. The ability to think differently from others is what will make you stand out in your workspace. Adopting a sustained habit of practicing mindfulness will change your perspective of work.

Another benefit of mindfulness is its capability to build empathy in your mind. Building empathy will prevent draining your mind with judgement for yourself or others around you. An empathetic approach can build sensitivity and therefore help in the formulation of more practical solutions for workplace issues.

During your 5-minute breaks after 55 minutes of deep focus incorporate a simple mindfulness walk or breathing session.

Build a Spartan-like Mindset

The Spartans were ancient Greek warriors who were famous for their mental and physical strength. They were taken from their parents as 10-year-old boys and spent all their time training mentally and physically. They used to run ten miles barefoot in groups with water in their mouths. At the end of the run everyone had to spit their water out and whoever had the most at the end would win. They were given a thin tunic and slept outside year-round, during the heat of summer and the blistering cold winters.

Building the mindset of an ancient spartan warrior will tremendously increase our threshold for maintaining focus and work quality throughout the work day. Mentioned below are the best ways to program your body and mind to withstand all hurdles that come your way.

Focus on Your Strengths Not Weakness'

For building focus like a Spartan, you must engage your strengths directly. The best way to overcome apprehension is to remind yourself that every situation can be fixed by awakening your dormant skills. You only find a solution to your problems once you believe in your abilities. Remind yourself of all the past fears you have overcome through sheer resilience and talent.

To become as resilient as a Spartan, you need to build your own identity around being a strong individual. Appreciate yourself and write down all the tough circumstances you have overcome. Instead of the details of the circumstance, focus on your response to it.

Direct your thinking to positive achievements of the past and write down the steps you took to adjust to changing circumstances. When you write your strengths down and how you can utilize them – you give your mind hope and confidence to succeed. You will find internal guidance that will keep you inspired. Set a standard for yourself and ignore what the rest of society is doing.

Once you are aware of your strengths, you will be well equipped to use them again. Avoid repressing the existence of uncomfortable memories. Such a psychological response, does not let us work through these with emotions effectively. In this process, pent up emotions can suppress your ability to overcome tough situations in the future. When you remind yourself how you overcame past trauma, you also reorient your mind to trusting itself.

Spartans were great warriors who succeeded through planning and discipline. You must plan on building your new identity as a strong warrior and effective planner who harnesses their mental energy to get the best results. Once you have clarity on your dormant skills and the new talents you want to acquire to succeed – you will be unstoppable for future obstacles.

Experiment with Intermittent Fasting

The practice of intermittent fasting facilitates the strategic skipping of meals for physical and mental fitness once or twice a week. When you train yourself to endure slight hunger for longer periods, you build endurance for tough situations. Think of yourself as a lion that is on the hunt – you are inspired, focused, motivated, and ready to capture your prey. With a mindset like that, you will conquer work challenges that come your way. Make sure to slowly build yourself up to this. Fasting can clear your mind, and improve cognitive functioning.

A paper in 2018 by Nature Reviews Neuroscience concludes that consistent fasting induces metabolic switching from using carbohydrates to ketones as fuel followed by a period of recovery will "optimize brain function and resilience". This promotes neuroplasticity and resistance to brain injuries or diseases. Our bodies are designed to go under a caloric deficit once a while, to force our bodies into ketosis which will grow new neural connections.

As an added bonus, like a Spartan at war, you will train your mind to be ready to achieve your goals despite physical desires such as hunger or pain that potentially can set you back.

Our ancestors often went to sleep and woke up hungry then had to go hunt for their prey. However, take this knowledge with a grain of salt, many people need to eat at least small amounts of calories at regular intervals in order to maintain focus especially if the individual is underweight, excessively stressed or sleep deprived. The easiest way to incorporate intermittent fasting into your life is to drink coffee with MCT oil in the morning and wait as long as you can until you notice your mental energy draining. Don't push yourself too far in the beginning, the idea is to slowly build up endurance over time and to ensure a full recovery with extra sleep and calories after. Don't sacrifice your immediate mental energy by going for too long without food especially if you are working on an important project. Be tactical with this knowledge because this is what will give you a cognitive boost and will increase your overall threshold for comfort.

Cold Showers for Willpower and Concentration

The sensation of a strong cold shower can wake you up to face your fears with a sharp and agile mind. The hit of piercing cold water in the morning will build your tolerance for uncomfortable situations. The largest benefit of cold water is your mind is immediately focused on the present moment. Practicing forcing yourself into focus with cold water is a life changing way to kickstart your journey to deep concentration.

When you wake up to an extremely cold shower in the morning daily, the problems at work will not seem so huge anymore – you have conquered the most difficult part of your day already. When you calm your body down on a biological level in a state of stress or discomfort then when psychological stress or discomfort enters your mind you are already trained in the art of relaxing and handling stress.

Acclimatizing yourself to the extreme discomfort of a cold shower on a winter morning will build your willpower and tolerance for stress. Begin with a lukewarm shower. After five minutes - lower the temperature of the water and keep slowly lowering until it is barely tolerable without shivering. It will not be pleasant at first, but the point is to build your mental endurance to withstand anything. Like mentioned earlier, Spartans existed in harsh conditions and therefore succeeded in conquering whatever wars they waged. You are aiming to build the same unflinching willpower that Spartans had through cold shower mind training. The moment the water hits you, you will be unable to think about anything else. You will be focused on the moment of the water running over you and put you in a deep state. When your brain is in survival mode it is not thinking about the past or future but only the present.

The goal of this activity is to be uncomfortable yet relaxed. Warm up the water before you start to shiver or gasp for air. If you push yourself too far you risk getting sick. The goal is to slowly increase our ability to relax in a physiological uncomfortable situation. Talk to your health care professional before pursuing cold showers.

Lift Weights

When you train yourself to lift adequately heavy weights for your personal fitness level at least three to four times a week, you will feel stronger and more capable of handling challenges. Your mind is trained to concentrate deeply despite the stressful situation of performing the heavy lift with perfect form.

Lifting weights will also give you a Spartan-like physique and boost your self-confidence. Just like cold showers, the difficulty of the task will nudge you to deal with workplace problems without fear, only concentration.

The real aim is to train your body into building better cognition. Athletes not only practice their sport but indulge in many other exercises to build better willpower, focus, and precision. Pushing your mind and muscles to grow through a combination of weight training and cardio ultimately strengthens your mind's ability to perform a difficult task for a long period. It also will increase your future threshold for sustaining attention.

Face your Fears

It is not uncommon to watch people let go of their life goals because they fear failure or risk. Like a Spartan, you need to face your fears. Start by writing them down and imagining what could happen if you gained the courage to tackle that new career, business or promotion.

Take a sheet of paper and divide it into three columns. Write your fear in the first column. Write the consequence of you acting on your fear in the second column. For instance, your fear is quitting your career for a new better or higher paying one, and the possible consequence is the fear of the unknown. Use the third column to write down what would happen if you never acted on your fear. Usually the regret of not acting on your dreams is scarier than the original fear ever will be. When you have the internal debate from your mind written on paper it will be far easier to see the benefits of taking that risk.

Decrease Resistance

Our reactions to adverse circumstances determine our fate– by reciting affirmations; you train yourself to accept the positive or negative that comes your way. This decreases resistance on our part and allows us to go with the flow. Use the belief system exercise from chapter 1 to help you with this. Add a new affirmation to your list for when you are dealing with challenging circumstances. For example, tell yourself, "this is easy, this is fun, I am strong", etc. This transforms your brain from the victim mentality to the empowered, focused and driven mentality. The act of programming your thoughts to be positive more frequently is called positive autosuggestion. It's all about perspective because if you see a task as daunting and heavy, your mind will immediately feel fatigued, and you won't be able to work effectively. But, if you see it as fun and easy, you will convince your mind to not see the task as a burden, ultimately making the obstacle shrink.

See your career as an adventure or journey to fulfill. This way, the tasks and problems you encounter will seem like things to be conquered and beaten – this motivates us to work harder and concentrate deeper. Fall in love with your journey to success so you can enjoy every moment and let the pieces fall into place.

Learn to accept your circumstances because when we try to resist, we waste a lot of mental energy. Famous psychologist Carl Jung always promoted the power of acceptance: "What we resist will not only persist but will grow in size." When we resist, we end up holding onto negative emotions like anger, sorrow, and grief, and slowly we become addicted to these limiting thoughts and wrap our identity around them. This lack of awareness and not dealing with our feelings ends up impeding your growth.

Resistance is fighting your reality and futilely trying to change it to your desired result. This chapter is about endurance but don't mistake brute force as a substitute for working intelligently.

Trying to cram our perception of reality into the box of what we want takes much energy – it requires us to shy away from our emotions, protest against them, and suppress them. The purpose of emotion is to help us understand and come to terms with what is happening to us. To avoid the potentially painful might seem like the right option, but in reality, we will be sacrificing our ability to handle a variety of obstacles in the future.

Impulse Control

Human beings are driven by their desires and, therefore, are impulsive creatures. Avoid unconscious negative behavior from impulses such as talking too much, gossiping, impulse shopping or eating. We all have immediate desires that we want to fulfill, but we have to exercise control, or our desires take control of us.

A great way to impulse control is to use urge surfing as a tool to disperse the desire. Urge surfing is a technique where you let your urges and desires build-up, imaging them like a giant wave, riding the feelings out and examining your thoughts from a third person perspective. Why do you have this urge? What will happen if I succumb to this urge? Will it make me happier or more fulfilled? This technique was developed by research scientist Sarah Bowen and is based on her theory that urges end up passing whether we act on them or not. You trick your brain into feeling the reward without completing the behavior. So, even though you can't control what impulses you have, you can exercise control over what you do about them. Her participants were addicted to smoking, and Bowen invited them to her lab, then asked them to take a pack of cigarettes in their hands, open it, smell the cigarette and use urge surfing to exercise control over their desire to smoke. All participants who regularly practiced urge surfing were able to resist the temptation of the cigarette. Slowly, they were able to eliminate their urge to smoke and experienced a positive mood shift.

Summary

With a proper plan and tool kit strengthening your threshold for discomfort is not only feasible but easier than you imagine. However, all of these exercises can lead to burnout if done for too many days in a row. Utilize breaks more and consider starting a mental health journal to keep your thoughts and emotions in the conscious before they get out of hand. Through focusing on your strengths, intermittent fasting, cold showers, facing your fears, working smart not hard, decreasing resistance, mindfulness and urge surfing are game changing and have a snowball effect when used together on your journey of focusing deep.

Action Steps

- Increase your deep focus blocks incrementally every week.
- Push yourself physically with exercise 3-4 times a week. Sustain your focus despite the physical discomfort.
- Experiment with turning the shower nozzle on cold for 1 minute. Time yourself and increase your cold-water time every week by 30 seconds.
- Keep your self-talk in check by reviewing the belief system exercise from Chapter 1.
- Keep logging in your mental health journal to avoid burnout. You may also use your productivity and sleep tracking journals to access why you feel burnt out. Work on slowly increasing the amount of daily challenges and pull back temporarily when it becomes too much.

PHASE 3: MIND HACKING & ADVANCED FOCUS TRAINING SECRETS YOU NEED TO KNOW

11

MIND HACKING – DECODING DOPAMINE

"In diving to the bottom of pleasure, we bring up more gravel than pearls."

HONORE DE BALZAC

Pleasure Fasting

Californian psychiatrist Dr. Cameron Sepah coined the term 'dopamine fasting' or 'dopamine detox' as a method for handling addictions. Dopamine fasting is a technique involving abstinence from pleasure-inducing activities for short periods. The term has very little to do with fasting or dopamine literally. People who use this technique are attempting to rest and reset their brains. The idea is to interrupt the brain's reward system. Dopamine is only one chemical in this system, however one cannot fast from a neurochemical. Pleasure fasters attempt to limit exciting food, internet, social media, and some even talking. Hardcore practitioners have often taken this method too far by avoiding human contact. Even to go as far as to not make direct eye contact with people, arguing that an eye contact is a form of human connection which the brain craves and rewards. This is a misunderstanding and there is no reason to deprive ourselves of something good for our health. After the end of the fasting period, detoxers feel a revitalization of enthusiasm for otherwise boring activities, heightening the amount of joy they extract from them. This technique gives our brain a tolerance break from overstimulation which greatly helps our ability to focus for long periods on career work.

To properly understand this method and to execute it well, you need to understand how dopamine affects the brain. Dopamine is a hormone and a neurotransmitter. It carries signals that are passed between neurons, thereby directing the collective behavior of the brain cells. Quite a few networks in the brain are dependent on dopamine for their functioning. One of those networks is especially relevant to the fasting technique. The mesolimbic reward pathway is an evolutionary pathway in the brain stem. This part of the brain is associated with survival. The ventral tegmental area projects to the nucleus accumbens, which play a role in rewards. There is a common misconception that postdoctoral researcher Arif Hamid at Brown University sheds light on with dopamine. Dopamine does not trigger pleasure, but it actually triggers the desire to do a task and the enjoyment you expect from it. Dopamine, therefore, coordinates how different parts of the brain react to inputs and information.

The term 'dopamine fasting' can be a little misleading because it is physically impossible and not healthy to eliminate dopamine from your body. Instead I will refer to it as pleasure fasting. This is also not the goal of a dopamine fast. The goal, instead, is to reduce or eliminate the time for which the brain engages in indulgent behavior that can be distracting or even problematic. If you are a ferocious social media scroller, your brain will experience the 'reward' sensation every time you use social media. When done frequently, the brain will recognize and register the pathway by which the reward is attained, and will even send dopamine to the reward pathway if it suspects that you will soon use social media.

With time, two problems emerge. Firstly, with the triggers for reward becoming more numerous, you are likely to spend even more time on social media because there is a longer sensation of pleasure. Secondly, when the brain gradually becomes used to excessive surges of dopamine, it transforms its response. The receptors that respond to dopamine are made weaker with excessive usage. Immediately after you stop using social media, your brain has fewer dopamine receptors than people who don't use social media that often. Decreased receptivity also means that you will need to spend more time on social media to attain the same level of dopamine that you received in earlier usages.

Pleasure fasting resets all these pathways and balances them out. In traditional psychological vocabulary, detoxing is used as a strategy to help individuals who are dealing with addiction to drugs and other substances. However, as many psychologists report, the obsession with food, sex, or social media shows symptoms which are pathologically equivalent to drug addiction.

Even though Internet and video game addictions are yet to be medically recognized as equivalent to drug use, their symptoms and treatments often overlap because of their similar nature. It is important to remember, however, that unlike drugs, a lot of pleasure-inducing activities are good ways to relax if they are done in controlled proportions. For a healthy psyche, small amounts of indulgence are not only appropriate, but it is also necessary. Pleasure fasts must be used only while dealing with an obsessive habit or lack of motivation in general. By getting comfortable with boredom and discomfort, you will transform your goal-oriented work into a fun, more pleasure inducing activity.

Why Pleasure Fast?

There are many reasons to pleasure fast. It is very easy to get lost in the momentum of your life, losing sight of your larger goals and dreams; a dopamine fast can help reset your priorities. By gaining control over your impulses, you can attain self-respect and the respect of others. Sometimes your negative habits affect your loved ones more than they affect you. Fasting helps you to reevaluate the value of personal relationships in your life. It also increases your overall satisfaction with life because every small reward will give you more joy. You will be able to process your pain better by removing distraction. Many times, natural negative emotions are stored up or repressed and can cause subconscious frustration. Pleasure fasts are a great way to come to terms with any hidden emotions.

How to Pleasure Fast

Pleasure fasts have a pretty straightforward implementation plan. You have to eliminate all digital screens (phones, laptops, and computers) and also any auditory stimulation like music, audiobooks or podcasts. You cannot read, shop, indulge in hot showers and unhealthy food. Instead consume simple, nourishing foods like brown rice and water. With all your freed-up time, meditate, take a nature walk, write, reflect and practice breathing exercises. A dopamine fast can be performed for anytime between a few hours to a full day based on your goals and practicality with work and family.

A dopamine fast is not a mindless activity. To get the most out of your fast, you must actively confront your fears and anxieties without shying away from them. Once you identify your pain, write it down, and trace its source.

Here is a writing exercise to perform. Ask yourself the following questions:

- Do I feel uncomfortable today? Is my discomfort more physical or emotional?
- Why do I feel this way? Try to not blame external circumstances, focusing more on your responses and issues.
- What are the actions that I have been taking or not taking to cause this feeling?
- What are the three things that I can do tomorrow to fix these shortcomings?
- What would my life look like if I didn't do these three things tomorrow? Describe the worst-case scenario that can emerge if I continue my current habits.
- What would my life be like if I did implement these three solutions tomorrow? Describe the best-case scenario.

Along with fasting 1-2 full days a year it is important to incorporate a few techniques into your daily life. View small scale pleasure fasting and embracing boredom as a lifestyle. Practice whenever an opportunity to be bored arises. When you are stuck in traffic or waiting in line for lunch, try to actively refrain from checking your phone and, instead, spend some time introspecting about your day and future goals. This will not only make your mind calmer; it will also help you connect your reward pathways to deep focus blocks rather than the next novel stimulus.

Summary

The world today is filled with distractions that are so easily available and is incredibly easy to become hooked to them. These distractions are also never-ending, which means that you can spend your entire life in a world of illusion without ever accomplishing your goals. While a life full of distractions is comfortable, indulgent, and easy, it will never help you follow your passions and discover your purpose. To attain the best version of yourself, you need to shed the desire for comfort and try to have the experiences of your dreams instead of finding comfortable alternatives.

For example, if you want to travel, instead of binge-watching travel shows, work hard, save money and do smaller trips yourself until you can afford larger trips. If you enjoy athletics, play sports instead of overly watching sports. If you want to find a partner, try to become the best version of yourself instead of watching porn to satiate temporary desire. None of the activities mentioned above are inherently wrong, but you must be careful with them because they have the potential to turn into dream destroying obsessions. The larger idea behind all these choices is that you want to stop living vicariously through someone else's dream and start working on actually fulfilling your own wildest dreams.

"Punishment of desire is the agony of unfulfillment"

HERMES TRISMEGISTUS, POIMANDRES

Bio-Hacking with Isochronic Tones

One of the most cutting edge and contemporary to date methods for igniting neuroplasticity is isochronic tones. Isochronic tones are frequencies that switch on and off at a regular rate. Even though this sounds simple, listening to isochronic tones has proven to do wonders to tune your brain into the state you desire using brainwave entrainment. While listening to isochronic tones, the brainwaves - which are formed as a result of the neurons exchanging information – attune themselves to the pace of frequencies and synchronize with their vibrations. This means that brain activity can be calmed down or increased at your own will, which potentially unlocks the key to owning your mind in the present. Neuroplasticity unlocks the key for future mental growth. This can also be incredibly helpful while dealing with stressful situations at work or in your personal life. Sound therapy is gaining popularity worldwide rapidly. Isochronic tones have proven to work better than the older but more famous binaural beats. Binaural beats have been popular brain entrainment therapy for years now and were discovered in 1839 by German researcher Heinrich Wilhelm Dove. They revolve around your brain adopting the difference in the frequencies between the right and left ear. Isochronic tones work on a much more evidence-based principle. Their effects and benefits are studied using EEGs, a test used to track the electrical activity in the brain.

Nearly two dozen independent, peer-reviewed, placebo-controlled studies conducted between the years 1979-2012 show a vast range of cognitive and behavioral benefits that can be attained with the help of isochronic tones to temporarily alter brain waves. They can be used to fine-tune your focus and memory. They are useful for insomniacs to develop healthy sleeping patterns or to start a power napping habit. On the other hand, it can be used during a procrastination period to trigger the brain into the deep state. The more frequently you listen to isochronic tones, the more familiar the sound will become as the brain becomes used to the pattern. Thus, with every use, your ability to focus deeper will increase using the power of neuroplasticity.

Use isochronic tones that switch between multiple beta frequencies between 13hz-30hz for maximum concentration. These beta wave frequencies are associated with increasing cognitive functioning, language processing, retrieval of semantic memory and sentence structuring according to many professors of neuroscience.

Summary

The usage of isochronic tones differs slightly from binaural beats since they don't require headphones like binaural beats do. They are easily available on the internet for free, on video streaming services, and independent websites. Access and set them up in your office or home space for immediate relaxation and focus. Nevertheless, just like every other therapy technique, you have to keep an open mind for them to work. If you take a negative and disbelieving attitude in an isochronic tone session, you will not feel the benefits of it even though EEGs have proven their effectiveness.

Action Steps

- Plan a pleasure fast for 1-2 days a year.
- Keep a pleasure fast journal and do the writing exercise.
- Be mindful about filling idle time with any activity that isn't identified as a priority in your life.

12

BRAIN TRAINING EXERCISES TO BUILD MONK-LIKE FOCUS

Training your brain is like upgrading hardware of a computer – you simply have to add more working memory or RAM with neuroplasticity to boost your IQ. This way, you can have control over your mind; you get to pick what the efficiency level of your mind is. As you train your mind your brain builds new neural pathways and stimulates neuron regeneration which strengthens neural pathways so that it functions more efficiently in every way. A normal human brain can hold about 3 to 5 chunks of different information at a single moment; my aim in this chapter is to help you increase this capacity.

Our brain's ability to hold more information is essential because all cognitive tasks require our brains to juggle and organize different forms of information. According to a research paper by the University of Missouri, psychological scientist Nelson Cowan, human adults can hold onto only seven different types of information at a given time. So, if you give anybody more than 7 chunks of information and ask them to recall all of them in any given order, they won't be able to remember more than 7 usually.

Our ability to store more memory allows us to have more meaningful encounters and situations. It not only increases what we can do in a given moment but also substantially impacts how much of our social environment we absorb and learn from. The larger the storage base we have, the more we see, hear, learn and retain. This allows us to generate even more meaning in our lives leading to cherishing every moment. It also helps us to switch between tasks more efficiently since our brain will handle new information without reducing cognitive ability. Our brain tends to get cluttered by multiple chunks of information we get from a single task, and even when we switch from one task to another, there is still some attentional residue left behind. But, with a large storage base, this residue doesn't impact the new task you are starting with as much, allowing you to work with a fresh mind. Attention residue is basically like having extra tabs open on your browser that just suck up the processing energy of your computer. It blocks your working memory if you don't have a lot of space available to hold information.

Before we dive deep into training our brains we must understand the difference between concentration exercises and meditation.

Meditation vs. Concentration Exercises

Both of these techniques sound similar, but they are quite different from each other. Meditation is all about letting your thoughts go by not trying to control them. This allows you to feel more tranquil by not attaching yourself to any one thought. Being more connected and aware of your senses. Concentration, on the other hand, is about taming the mind and restricting its ability to wander anywhere. To concentrate means to be completely focused on one place, object, or thought until everything else melts from existence including one's sense of self. In this state of mind, you have complete control, and therefore, can direct your cognitive power to whatever you desire. Meditation is about synergistically being aware while concentration is about singularity. Beginner meditation is about being aware of the mind while concentration is about shutting everything else out. You garner the capacity to control what is allowed to enter your mind and what occupies your attention.

Starting with concentration exercises before moving into learning meditation is the path of least resistance from my personal experience. There are many benefits of meditation. According to a study by the University of South Carolina at Charlotte, meditation improved the critical cognitive skills of participants. What the researchers noticed was that just after four days of participants practicing mindfulness for 20 minutes each day, their cognitive skills improved, and their thinking became sharper. The participants were told to simply relax and focus on their breathing. If any random thought came to their mind, they were supposed to acknowledge the thought and let it go.

We must learn the basics of concentration before we move onto mindfulness, awareness and meditation to build a baseline level of focus.

Main Concentration Exercise: Starting with the Basics of Complete Singular Attention.

Start with just 1 minute of complete focus on 1 thing, such as your breath, a single affirmation or specific sensation. Completing this 1 minute of unwavering concentration will be surprisingly challenging for most individuals. Do this exercise every day, adding 1 minute every week. Restart or scale back the time if you don't deter thoughts and distractions. Instead of resisting thoughts and distractions simply replace them with attention to your breathing. Don't be hard on yourself if you can't even do 1 minute. You are not alone and the majority of western society does not have this skill yet. Try your best to hone and tame your mind.

Dual N Back Game

This is a game to help you increase your working memory by making it possible for you to process more information at once in your immediate concentration. A study done by John Hopkins University found that the brain could be trained like any other part of the body through constant hard work. The researchers found that the group that practiced the dual-n-back game recorded a 30% improvement in their working memory. The game also changed the prefrontal cortex structure of the brain, which is responsible for higher learning and concentration.

Dual N Back is a game-based memory sequence that tests the participants' ability to remember auditory and visual stimuli that constantly changes. The participants would hear letters while squares flashed on a grid in front of them. All they had to do was try to remember if the letter they heard and the square they saw were the same as the ones from the previous round. The test was slowly made harder, and they had to remember letters and squares from 3 to 4 rounds back.

The purpose of this was to train the working memory to remember as much information as possible. Improvement in working memory allows you to learn new things faster and process them more efficiently so that no information is lost. Hence, dual-n-back is the best technique since it's backed by the most high-quality research.

Visualization Exercises

Visualizations help to improve your creativity, build a photogenic memory, and heighten concentration to new extremes. Learning how to visualize is simple, and anybody can do it. Most of us use visual images to store information. Many memory experts recommend turning the things you want to remember into symbols and chunk them together so that you more easily access them by just imagining the visual you created.

Here are some general tips for all visualization exercises:

- Relax: If you want to form mental imagery, start by scanning your body to look for any tensions. Relax your mind and your body to open your mental vision.

- Calm eyes: Straining your eyes reduces the muscles' ability to form images.

- Opening and closing eyes: Most individuals get the best results from closed eyes however periodically opening the eyes can fluctuate light and potentially make visuals come easier.

- Playfulness: You have to push your inner creativity to allow your mind's eye to become better at visualizing. Don't force yourself, relax and be in a state of flow.

Object Cloning Visualization

- Draw a basic shape and color it in on a piece of paper, such as a triangle. Look at the triangle until it becomes clear in your mind.

- Close your eyes. Have the basic shape in your mind, then slowly watch it turn clockwise. After a minute, make it turn counter-clockwise. Then add two of the same shape and repeat the process but tracking multiple shapes now.

- Try placing an object in front of you, such as an apple, or flame on a candle. Close your eyes and practice seeing it, vividly and intricately detailed. Don't be discouraged if the image fades from your imagination, simply open your eyes and start over. Over time upgrade to new complex objects that will challenge you.

Photographic recall

Vividly imagine a place with all your willpower. Take a picture of a place, pictures of nature work the best or a picture that you're familiar with. Now, close your eyes and recreate the photograph in your head. Try to recreate every aspect of the photo; start with the background, try to home in on the different aspects of the background like the color gradation, places, and geographic markers. Now, think of the others colors in the photos. By trying to remember and differentiate small details your visualization will become stronger. Have the physical or digital picture in front of you in case you mentally lose the image so you can open your eyes and start over. After you open your eyes, check the actual photograph and rectify all the mistakes you made. Continue this exercise until you are able to create an absolutely identical image of the photo in your head.

Relive your day

At the end of your day take a moment to lay down and visualize every moment of your day step by step. Start visualizing from the very beginning of your day. The second you opened your eyes to the moment you lay down. By reliving your day step by step, you'll be able to practice visualizing your own synthetic experiences with greater effectiveness. You'll be able to apply this skill to visualizing yourself focusing on a challenge at work, in turn making it easier to accomplish.

Mentally write your name

Write your name on a piece of paper in front of you. Close your eyes and watch yourself repeat the action slowly. Most people can only see visually one letter at a time; your end goal will be to imagine as many letters as you can together. This exercise will ideally not take you more than 30 seconds.

Watching thoughts from the third-person perspective

Try to disassociate yourself from your thoughts by visualizing your thoughts from the third person. Imagine yourself sitting by the edge of a river, as a thought enters your mind watch it float by on a log or leaf individually. Eventually, you will feel a sense of tranquility that will bleed into the rest of your life. When we are aware of our thoughts, we will become extremely better at reprogramming them for focus.

Counting down from 100 to 0

Visualize the number 100 in front of you. Countdown to 0, visualizing each number vividly. Restart if you lose the mental picture.

Watch the clock

Another exercise to increase concentration is to watch the second hand of the clock for 5 minutes.

Physical Exercises

Physical exercises train the brain to naturally take control of the body completely and respond faster. It also strengthens the synapses that connect your mind, body and motor regions of the brain. This will help you by increasing your concentration, making attention more seamless and dynamic.

Hold a glass of water

Simply grab a clear glass of water and fill it half full. While holding the glass of water extend your arm all the way. Stare at the water and keep the top completely still for 1 minute. This exercise can be challenging but highly effective.

Sit completely still

Find a comfortable place to sit and practice not moving a single muscle for 1 minute. Gradually increase your time. Learning to sit completely still will greatly improve your concentration and willpower.

Make a Fist

Have your hand out flat, palm up and your elbow hanging at your side. Slowly and deliberately curl your fingers forming your hand into a fist. The goal is to squeeze tightly and be present completely. Then elevate your fist towards your shoulder curling your arm. Squeeze your bicep. Slowly undo the curl, then undo the fist until you reach the same palm open and flat position. Be honest with yourself, once you can fully concentrate on one arm experiment with doing both arms at the same time without wavering in concentration. The beauty of this exercise is it can be done from almost anywhere.

The Concentration Lifestyle

Concentration is not simply a state that we pursue but a moment by moment conscious choice. Every single action we do throughout the day can be intentional and deliberate. This is the secret to skyrocketing your ability to focus deeply. Deep focus is a lifestyle. Every gifted moment of being alive is an opportunity to be fully present in this very moment down to the millisecond. Every moment of being alive is a reward and a chance to practice intention over your thoughts and actions. A state where you are aware of everything around you and yourself simultaneously. There are many ways we can practice being more focused in our daily activities.

When in conversation with someone, to appear as an attentive listener:

- Avoid looking around
- Instead of thinking about what you're going to say next, try to summarize what they told you.

When watching videos online, try not to read the comment section until you are done with the video. When you are eating, avoid watching tv, listening to podcasts or music. Focus on the textures and flavors of the delicious food. Read physical or digital books. The more activities that we do solely by themselves and intentionally the more our focus will exponentially grow.

Action Steps

- Set time aside on your days off and, at the end of every day, in your calendar for focus training.
- Download a meditation time tracking app to track your timed concentration exercise. Make sure it allows you to take a few quick notes on how you felt about the concentration session or keep a meditation/concentration journal.

Your daily regimen will consist of:

- The main concentration exercises.
- Dual N Back app on your phone or software on your computer.
- 1 visual or physical exercise. Change this exercise to a new one every 2 weeks. Exercises are most effective when novel.
- Don't overwhelm yourself. 1 minute a day will change your life over time using the compound effect.

As an independent author with a small budget to get my voice heard, book reviews are my livelihood.

If you enjoyed reading this book as much as I enjoyed writing it, I would appreciate if you left your honest feedback. You can do so by visiting the review page for this book on Amazon or scanning the QR code below.

I adore hearing from my readers and personally read every review. I look forward to hearing from you!

http://www.amazon.com/gp/customer-reviews/write-a-review.html?asin=B08929W45F

With love,

Chandler

AFTERWORD

"Quench your soul, capture your focus, and you'll never work a day in your life."

CHANDLER KITCHING

Knowledge of your mind is your greatest tool for mastering your concentration. Neuroplasticity allows you to have unlimited intelligence and masterful focus. Your brain is unlimited, you can push it to remember more, transform, and through repetition, make concentration your natural state of being. The subconscious mind must be trained to be an endless source of creative imagination through visualization and affirmations. Focus on your feelings of deep gratitude. You have to be deliberate about your thoughts and intentional about your beliefs. You are a masterful concentrator. Imagine yourself attaining that promotion, conquering your freedom goals and loving the process.

You have to build the right habits to turn yourself into a deep focus machine. By building schedules and routines, you will streamline your day. The biggest hurdle you will face is deterring and handling distractions. By understanding distractions and what kind of distractions you are most susceptible to you can train yourself to focus on the tasks at hand. If you are participating in an activity that leaves you feeling drained afterwards that isn't required by your work avoid it like the black plague.

Your workspace is a sacred space of devout deep attention. Treat it as such and only keep possessions in your vicinity that hold purpose. Prioritize intention over possessions. How you spend your time and arrange your space determines the length and depth of your attention span. If it's not your office or desk, you must discover a separate space where disturbances are less.

Your biology can be upgraded to boost your baseline cognitive and executive functions. You must hone in on your sleeping patterns, water intake, diet, and concentration exercises. Your mind is an organ, and it requires maintenance through regimental training. Nootropics increase your memory storage, strengthen brain synapses, and boost cognitive function to further increase your baseline focus level.

Once you can sharpen your thinking process by hacking your mind and body, you have to take the next step of learning the fundamentals of focusing deep. You must plan out your day, build focus blocks, and take deep relaxation breaks seriously. Utilize necessary distraction to ensure that you don't waste time or energy. Use moments of day dreaming to think creatively, reflect on your work and solve your problems. The best way to focus is by learning how to ritually trigger entering the deep state to unleash our ultimate focus. By immersing yourself into your work and becoming one with it, you will create a connection with your work that ensures that your obstacles fall easier, and mountains will be moved.

Clearing mental clutter and only allowing the essential into our minds is the path of least resistance. Use all your mental energy towards focusing deep on goal-oriented work. Use your downtime to relax deeply to replenish your mind and always be ready for the next work challenge.

While keeping our energy levels high we must simultaneously increase our focus thresholds by embracing discomfort. Slowly push yourself daily and allow your mind to recover and rest fully to avoid burnout while growing. The cold shower technique is pivotal in teaching you to harness discomfort towards increasing your focus.

The advanced mind training techniques mentioned in this book are the key to unlocking the brain's potential. We are all driven by pleasure, but by using tricks like pleasure fasting, we will learn to discover deep satisfaction from our work.

Practice your main concentration exercise, Dual N Back and one visual or physical exercise daily for insane concentration gains. Pair that with understanding how concentration is a lifestyle, not just a practice and you are unstoppable. By practicing intentionality moment by moment, you will reach a mindful state where you are always rewarded by the present and use your cognitive abilities to the maximum.

The end goal that I envisioned in the beginning of the book was to develop a full encompassing action plan that will deepen your concentration mastery. The deeply focused, prioritized and deliberate life will push a snowball of happiness down the mountain of your life, growing to the power of ten-second by second. We want to look back at our lives from our deathbed and relish in our accomplishments. We want to have deep gratitude and pride at how we lived our lives to the best of our abilities. Seizing every moment as if they were our last. By using the techniques mentioned in this book, you will undoubtedly develop a focus that will have you savoring life, grabbing every opportunity, and never regretting a lost moment. Concentration ensures that we will accomplish everything we desire without compromising our family, friends, passions and values.

As a society, the concentration lifestyle has the potential to help everyone experience the gratitude of being alive and will spark a global collective fulfillment. When we learn how to cherish the exquisite, and intricate finer details in life, our five senses light up, everything becomes alive, we experience deep relentless fulfillment and we maximize our potential as a species.

My Other Books You'll Love

Find Your Passion:

Discover Purpose & Live the Life of Your Wildest Dreams

The Art of Doing Nothing:

The No-Guilt Practical Burnout Recovery System for Busy Professionals

REFERENCES

Adams, A. J. (2009, December 3). Seeing is believing: The power of visualization. Psychology Today. https://www.psychologytoday.com/us/blog/flourish/200912/seeing-is-believing-the-power-visualization

Altrogge, S. (2019, March 21). Master your time: 5 daily scheduling methods to bring more focus to your day. Zapier. https://zapier.com/blog/daily-schedules-for-productivity/

American Psychological Association. (n.d.). Is Willpoweralimitedresource?[PDFfile]. https://www.apa.org/helpcenter/willpower-limited-resource.pdf

Asprey, D. (n.d.). Step 6: Upgrade your brain, improve your cognition. https://blog.daveasprey.com/upgrade-your-brain/

Babauta, L. (n.d.). Discomfort zone: How to master the universe. Zen Habits.

https://zenhabits.net/discomfort/

Brainworks. (n.d.). What is neuroplasticity?

https://brainworksneurotherapy.com/what-neuroplasticity

Barlow-Oregon, J. (2018, January 8). Gratitude journals may change our brains. Futurity.

https://www.futurity.org/writing-gratitude-charity-1648582/

Beilock, S. (2012, October 10). Want to be creative? Let your mind wander. Psychology Today.

https://www.psychologytoday.com/us/blog/choke/201210/want-be-creative-let-your-mind-wander

BrainMD Life. (2016, August 23). Focus on choline: Improvefocus&memory.BrainMD. https://brainmd.com/blog/focus-on-choline-improve-focus-memory/

Brooks, S. (2020, March 9). How acetyl-l-carnitine burns fat and powers the brain. Bulletproof. https://www.bulletproof.com/supplements/aminos-enzymes/acetyl-l-carnitine-benefits/

Bryce, E. (2019, November 9). How many calories can the brain burn by thinking? Live Science. https://www.livescience.com/burn-calories-brain.html

Canfield, J. (n.d.). Daily affirmations for positive thinking. https://www.jackcanfield.com/blog/practice-daily-affirmations/

Celine. (2017, October 12). Difference between concentration and meditation.

Cherry, K. (2019, August 8). 'Flow' Can Help You Achieve Goals. Verywell Mind

https://www.verywellmind.com/what-is-flow-2794768

Cleanwp. (2016, December 22). Springbrook sensory modulation series: Full spectrum lights. Springbrook Autism. Behavioral. Health. https://springbrookautismbehavioral.com/portfolio-item/springbrook-sensory-modulation-series-full-spectrum-lights/

Clear, J. (n.d.). How to build new habits by taking advantage of old ones. https://jamesclear.com/habit-stacking

Cohen, J. F. W., Gorski, M.T., Gruber, S. A., Kurdziel, L. B. F., & Rimm, E. B. (2016). The effect of healthy dietary consumption on executive cognitive functioning in children and adolescents: A systematic review. British Journal of Nutrition, 116(6), 989-1000. https://doi.org/10.1017/S0007114516002877

Cohut, M. (2019, November 2). How waste gets 'washed out' of our brains during sleep. Medical News Today. https://www.medicalnewstoday.com/articles/326896

Cools, R. (2008). Role of dopamine in the motivational and cognitive control of behavior. The Neuroscientist, 14(4), 381-395.
https://doi.org/10.1177/1073858408317009

Cowan, G. (2016, August 11). Lessons from Michael Phelps' extraordinary pre race ritual.
https://graemecowan.com.au/lessons-michael-phelps-extraordinary-pre-race-ritual/

Cowan, N. (2010). The magical mystery four: How is working memory capacity limited, and why? Current Directions in Psychological Science, 19(1), 51-57. doi: 10.1177/0963721409359277

David, P., Jung-Hyun, K., Brickman, J. S., Ran, W., & Curtis, C. M. (2014). Mobile phone distraction while studying. New Media and Society, 17(10), 1661-1679. https://doi.org/10.1177/1461444814531692

Davidson, C. N. (2011, November 13). The history of distraction, 4000 BCE to the present. https://www.cathydavidson.com/blog/the-history-of-distraction-4000-bce-to-the-present/

Davis, J. (2015, October 6). How background noise affects the way you work. Fast Company.

https://www.fastcompany.com/3051835/how-background-noise-affects-the-way-you-work

Dibra, S. (2014, October 7). Mindfulness can increase your concentration and lower stress. Penn State World CampusBlog.
https://blog.worldcampus.psu.edu/mindfulness-can-increase-your-concentration-and-lower-stress/

Diffenderfer, S. (n.d.). Grape seed extract: protector of brain cells and cognitive function.
https://www.sarahdiff.com/grapeseed-extract/

DifferenceBetween.net. (n.d.).

http://www.differencebetween.net/language/words-language/difference-between-concentration-and-meditation/

D'Mello, S. S., Chipman, P., & Graesser, A. (2007). Posture as a predictor of learner's affective engagement. Proceedings of the Annual Meeting of the Cognitive Science.Society,29(29).
https://escholarship.org/uc/item/7hs9v2hr

Duffy, J. (2018, May 15). Beyond decision fatigue: How managing decisions can help or hurt your productivity. Zapier. https://zapier.com/blog/decision-fatigue-productivity/

Dumont, T. Q. (1998). The Power of Concentration. [eBook edition]. Project Gutenberg.
http://www.gutenberg.org/cache/epub/1570/pg1570-images.html

Dye, L. (2011, October 4). Can you raise your IQ? Yes, ifyouthinkyoucan. ABCNews.
https://abcnews.go.com/Technology/raise-iq-mind-set-

matters-psychologists/story?id=14668170

Edblad, P. (n.d.). Urge surfing: How to break bad habits with mindfulness. https://patrikedblad.com/habits/urge-surfing/

Ervolino, B. (2017, October 19). Everybody is exhausted: Stress and social media are taking their toll. ChicagoTribune.
https://www.chicagotribune.com/lifestyles/health/ct-social-media-exhaustion-20171019-story.html

Fleyshgakker, J. (n.d.). 10 benefits to daydreaming! Lifehack. https://www.lifehack.org/279770/10-benefits-daydreaming

Etaugh, C. & Ptasnik, P. (1982). Effects of studying to music and post-study relaxation on reading comprehension. Perceptual and Motor Skills, 55(1), 141-142.

https://doi.org/10.2466/pms.1982.55.1.141

Godman, H. (2018, April 5). Regular exercise changes the brain to improve memory, thinking skills. Harvard HealthBlog.
https://www.health.harvard.edu/blog/regular-exercise-changes-brain-improve-memory-thinking-skills-201404097110

Graybiel, A. M. (2009). Basal ganglia: Habit. In L. R. Squire (Ed.), Encyclopedia of Neuroscience, (pp. 93-96). Academic Press.

Gregoire, C. (2016, March 18). The new science of the creative brain on nature. Outside. https://www.outsideonline.com/2062221/new-science-creative-brain-nature

Gregoire, C. (2017, January 9). Why silence is so good for your brain. HuffPost. https://www.huffpost.com/entry/silence-brain-benefits_n_56d83967e4b0000de4037004?guccounter=1

Hamilton, D. R. Using science to inspire. (2014, June 30).

https://drdavidhamilton.com/5-reasons-why-you-should-visualize/

Herrera, T. (2019, January 13). How to actually, truly focus on what you're doing. The New York Times.

https://www.nytimes.com/2019/01/13/smarter-living/how-to-actually-truly-focus-on-what-youre-doing.html

Hill, A. (2018, May 29). 12 Benefits of ginkgo biloba (plus side effects & dosage). Healthline. https://www.healthline.com/nutrition/ginkgo-biloba-benefits#section4

Horvath, A. T., Misra, K., Epner, A. K., & Cooper, G. M. (n.d.). Drug seeking and cravings: Addictions' effect on the brain's reward system. CenterSite. https://www.centersite.net/poc/view_doc.php?type=doc&id=48375&cn=1408

Hoyt, A. (n.d.) How multitasking works. HowStuffWorks. https://science.howstuffworks.com/life/inside-the-mind/human-brain/multitasking.htm

Janecic, P. (2020, April 14). The cold shower approach to developing mental toughness. Mind of Steel. https://themindofsteel.com/cold-shower/

Jha, A. (2007, March 9). Brain absorbs subliminal messages if not too busy. The Guardian.

https://www.theguardian.com/science/2007/mar/09/neuroscience.medicineandhealth

Karakolis, T., & Callaghan, J. P. (2014). The impact of sit–stand office workstations on worker discomfort and productivity: A review. Applied Ergonomics, 45(3), 799-806. https://doi.org/10.1016/j.apergo.2013.10.001

Kotler, S. (n.d.). Introduction to the optimized brain: A mini-workshop on flow states. https://www.stevenkotler.com/rabbithole/est-rerum-cum

Kotsopoulou, A. & Hallam, S. (2010). The perceived impact of playing music while studying: Age and cultural differences. Educational Studies, 36(4), 431-440. https://doi.org/10.1080/03055690903424774

Kotler, S. (n.d.). 8 steps to a world-class understanding of creativity (and how to hack it). https://www.stevenkotler.com/rabbithole/reiciendis-aut-perspiciatis-et-copy

O'Brien, S. (2018, May 14). 7 science-based benefits of MCT oil. Healthline. https://www.healthline.com/nutrition/mct-oil-benefits#section8

Oppong, T. (2018, June 6). How to build routines that conserve brainpower for high-level thinking. Medium. https://medium.com/@alltopstartups/how-to-build-routines-that-conserve-brainpower-for-high-level-thinking-82a0d3238f16

Lakhiani, V. (2018, August 6). 13 strategies to get in flow based on the latest research by Steven Kotler. https://blog.mindvalley.com/how-to-get-in-flow/?utm_source=blog

Lanese, N. (2019, November 19). Is there actually science behind 'dopamine fasting'? Live Science. https://www.livescience.com/is-there-science-behind-dopamine-fasting-trend.html

Lapidos, R. (2019, March 8). If you have zero attention span, sharpen your focus with these essential oils. Well And Good. https://www.wellandgood.com/good-looks/essential-oils-for-focus/

Leibman, P. Attention residue: The costly side effect of switchingtasks.Stronger Habits. https://strongerhabits.com/attention-residue/

Leprince-Ringuet, D. (2018, August 22). Here's scientific proof your brain was designed to be distracted. Wired. https://www.wired.co.uk/article/brain-distraction-procrastination-science

Lewis, J. (n.d.). Isochronic tones – How they work, the benefits and the research. Mind Amend. https://www.mindamend.com/brainwave-entrainment/isochronic-tones/

Martelli, M. (2015, February 1). How to visualize? Learn to create mental imagery – From scratch. UnchainMyBrain. https://unchainmybrain.com/learn-to-visualize/

Martelli, M. (2019, June 6). How mental imagery in sport can improve your performance. UnchainMyBrain. https://unchainmybrain.com/mental-imagery-in-sport/

Martynoga, B. (2016, June 18). How physical exercise makes your brain work better. The Guardian. https://www.theguardian.com/education/2016/jun/18/ho

w-physical-exercise-makes-your-brain-work-better

Mattson, M. P., Moehl, K., Ghena, N., Schmaedick, M., & Cheng, A. (2018). Intermittent metabolic switching, neuroplasticity and brain health. Nature Reviews Neuroscience, 19(2), 63-80. doi: 10.1038/nrn.2017.156

Mautz, S. (2019, April 14). Want to boost your productivity? Science says listen to music with these 6 Rules in mind. Inc.
https://www.inc.com/scott-mautz/science-says-you-get-astonishing-productivity-boosts-by-listening-to-music-

just-follow-these-6-rules.html

McKay, B., & McKay, K. (2019, March 4). 12 concentration exercises from 1918. Art of Manliness. https://www.artofmanliness.com/articles/12-concentration-exercises-from-1918/

Mills, P. R., Tomkins, S. C., Schlangen, L. J. M. (2007). The effect of high correlated colour temperature office lighting on employee wellbeing and work performance. Journal of Circadian Rhythms, 5, Article 2. doi:10.1186/1740-3391-5-2

National Sleep Foundation. (n.d.). How lack of sleep impacts cognitive performance and focus.

https://www.sleepfoundation.org/articles/how-lack-sleep-impacts-cognitive-performance-and-focus

Neal, D. T., Wood, W., Wu, M., & Kurlander, D. (2011). The pull of the past: When do habits persist despite conflict with motives? Personality and Social Psychology Bulletin, 37(11), 1428-1437. https://doi.org/10.1177/0146167211419863

Neurohacker Collective. (2018, May 25). Understanding

the function and benefits of huperzine A. https://neurohacker.com/understanding-the-function-and-benefits-of-huperzine-a

Newport, C. (2017, September 18). Approach Technology like the Amish
https://www.calnewport.com/blog/2017/09/18/approach-technology-like-the-amish/

Oshin, M. (2018, September 10). 9 ways multitasking is killing your brain and productivity, according to neuroscientists.Ladders.
https://www.theladders.com/career-advice/9-ways-multitasking-is-killing-your-brain-and-productivity-according-to-neuroscientists

Paredes, R. (2018, December 12). Lion's mane mushroom benefits: Boost memory, focus & mood with This noortropic bulletproof.
https://www.bulletproof.com/supplements/dietary-supplements/lions-mane-mushroom-benefits/

Raman, R. (2019, October 31). 7 emerging benefits of bacopa monnieri (brahmi). Healthline.
https://www.healthline.com/nutrition/bacopa-monnieri-benefits#8

Ranganathan, V. K., Siemionow, V., Liu, J. Z., Sahgal, V., & Yue, G. H. (2004). From mental power to muscle power--gaining strength by using the mind. Neuropsychologia, 42(7), 944-956. doi: 10.1016/j.neuropsychologia.2003.11.018

Reddy, S. (2013, September 2). The perfect nap: Sleeping is a mix of art and science. The Wall Street Journal. https://www.wsj.com/articles/the-perfect-nap-sleeping-is-a-mix-of-art-and-science-1378155665

Roomer, J. (2019, February 12). How to reach flow state (using 10 flow state 'triggers'). Medium. https://medium.com/personal-growth-lab/how-to-reach-flow-state-using-10-flow-state-triggers-473aa28dc3e5

Rosen, J. (2017, October 17). Johns Hopkins finds training exercise that boosts brain power. Johns Hopkins University. https://releases.jhu.edu/2017/10/17/johns-hopkins-finds-training-exercise-that-boosts-brain-power/

Rossen, J. (2019, March 7). Could you keep up with Theodore Roosevelt's ruthlessly efficient daily routine? MentalFloss. https://www.mentalfloss.com/article/576280/theodore-roosevelts-ruthlessly-efficient-daily-routine

Sasson, R. (n.d.). Concentration exercises for training and focusing the mind. Success Consciousness. https://www.successconsciousness.com/blog/concentration-mind-power/concentration-exercises/

Science Daily. (2009, May 12). Brain's problem-solving Function at work when we daydream.
https://www.sciencedaily.com/releases/2009/05/090511180702.htm

Science Daily. (2019, April 1). Physical activity may strengthen children's ability to pay attention. https://www.sciencedaily.com/releases/2009/03/090331183800.htm

Science Daily. (2010, April 19). Brief meditative Exercise helps cognition
https://www.sciencedaily.com/releases/2010/04/100414184220.html

Seger, C. A. & Spiering, B. J. (2011). A critical review of habit learning and the basal ganglia. Frontiers in Systems Neuroscience,5, Article 66. doi: 10.3389/fnsys.2011.00066

Seltzer, L. F. (2016, June 15). You only get more of what you resist—Why? Psychology Today. https://www.psychologytoday.com/us/blog/evolution-the-self/201606/you-only-get-more-what-you-resist-why

Shaffer, J. (2016). Neuroplasticity and clinical practice: Building brain power for health. Frontiers in Psychology, 7, 1118. doi: 10.3389/fpsyg.2016.01118

Söderlund, G. B. W., Sikström, S., Loftesnes, J. M., & Sonuga-Barke, E. J. (2010). The effects of background white noise on memory performance in inattentive school children. Behavioral and Brain Functions, 6, Article 55. doi: 10.1186/1744-9081-6-55

Sound of Sleep. (n.d.). White, pink, and brown noise: What'sthedifference? https://www.soundofsleep.com/2017/07/18/white-pink-brown-noise-whats-difference/

Sparks, C. (2018, February 26). 106: Triggers — The Key to Building and Breaking Habits. Medium. https://medium.com/@SparksRemarks/triggers-the-key-to-building-and-breaking-habits-fa8ed153ab0c

Squire, L. R., & Shrager, Y. (2008). Declarative memory system: Amnesia. Learning and Memory: A Comprehensive Reference, 3, 67-78.

https://doi.org/10.1016/B978-012370509-9.00118-2

Steidle, A., & Werth, L. (2013). Freedom from constraints: Darkness and dim illumination promote creativity. Journal of Environmental Psychology, 35, 67-80. https://doi.org/10.1016/j.jenvp.2013.05.003

Stone, C. (2019, November 18). 7 benefits of mindfulness in the workplace. GQR. https://www.gqrgm.com/7-benefits-of-mindfulness-in-the-workplace/

Stromberg, J. (2012, April 3). The benefits of daydreaming. Smithsonian Magazine. https://www.smithsonianmag.com/science-nature/the-benefits-of-daydreaming-170189213/

Suttie, J. (2018, February 14). How mind-wandering may be good for you. Greater Good Magazine. https://greatergood.berkeley.edu/article/item/how_mind_wandering_may_be_good_for_you

Thibodeaux, W. (2017, May 23). Create the ultimate creativity space. Inc. https://www.inc.com/wanda-thibodeaux/how-to-declutter-your-office-and-create-the-ultimate-creativity-space.html

Thorne, B. (2020, February 13). How distractions at work take up more time than you think. I Done This Blog. http://blog.idonethis.com/distractions-at-work/

Trapani, G. (2007, July 24). Jerry Seinfeld's productivity secret. Lifehacker. https://lifehacker.com/jerry-seinfelds-productivity-secret-281626

University of Pennsylvania Annenberg School for Communication. (2015, November 20). Study reveals the neural mechanics of self-affirmation. https://www.asc.upenn.edu/news-events/news/study-reveals-neural-mechanics-self-affirmation

University of California Davis Student Health and Counseling Services. (2015, December 2). Your brain on H2O. https://shcs.ucdavis.edu/blog/archive/healthy-habits/your-brain-h2o

Van De Walle, G. (2018, March 3). 7 science-backed health benefits of rhodiola rosea. Healthline. https://www.healthline.com/nutrition/rhodiola-rosea

Van Oudheusdena, L. J., & Scholteb H. R. (2002) Efficacy of carnitine in the treatment of children with attention-deficit hyperactivity disorder. Prostaglandins, Leukotrienes and Essential Fatty Acids, 67(1), 33-38. https://doi.org/10.1054/plef.2002.0378

Ward, S. (2019, December 1). 10 file management tips to keep your electronic files organized. The Balance SmallBusiness. https://www.thebalancesmb.com/computer-file-management-tips-2948083

Wim Hof Method. (n.d.). Benefits of cold showers. https://www.wimhofmethod.com/benefits-of-cold-showers

Wyone, D. P., & Wargocki, P. (2006). Room temperature effects on office work [PDF file]. In D. Clements-Croome. (Eds.), Creating the productive workplace. (2nd ed., pp. 181-189). Taylor & Francis. https://www.researchgate.net/publication/279190533_Creating_the_Productive_Workplace

Printed in Great Britain
by Amazon